SETS ON A SHOESTRING

How to Build Sets and Props on a Limited Budget

LAUREL WENSON

Copyright © 2019 by Laurel Wenson

All rights reserved.

No part of this book may be reproduced in any form or by any electronic or mechanical means, including information storage and retrieval systems, without written permission from the author, except for the use of brief quotations in a book review.

❧ Created with Vellum

*This book is lovingly dedicated to
every theater student I've
had the privilege of working with
over the years.
Thank you for being the CAKE!*

CONTENTS

Introduction	vii
1. The Set Building Tool Kit	1
2. Set Terminology	3
3. Basic Set Design	7
4. Flat Building with Cardboard	13
5. Indoor Settings	24
6. Outdoor Settings	39
7. Magical / Fantasy Settings	47
8. Homemade Indoor Props	53
9. Homemade food props	63
10. Homemade Outdoor Props	69
11. Homemade Fantasy / Magical Props	76
12. How much should the cast help?	91
13. The Use of Lighting and Sound	95
Appendix A — Photo Credits	97
Appendix B — Useful resources	98
Acknowledgments	99
About the Author	101

INTRODUCTION

For years I felt the sensation every time the curtain opened: set envy. The elaborate backdrops, the smoke machines, the trap doors, the costuming –all reflecting a budget that I could only dream about. Once the show started I'd get caught up in the magic and all would be fine. Sometimes the show would be phenomenal, and other times I'd head home thinking more about the set than the performance I saw.

That's when I realized that it wasn't the fancy sets that made a show memorable, but the actors on stage. And that's a good thing, because most of us who direct and produce musicals and plays with children and young adults don't have much to work with in terms of money and resources. If you've ever experienced "set envy", or stopped by the side of the road to pick a prop or set piece out of someone's trash, or got excited about cardboard and duct tape, then read on.

This book will explore the world of set building at the most basic level and answer questions like, "How do I make a street lamp?", or "Do I need a whole new backdrop for every scene?" After years of creating countless homemade props from recycled items and building sets from scratch, I've learned things that worked and things that didn't. I discovered resources that made production life easier, and learned to spend whatever money I DID have as wisely as I could to keep sets simple but functional. Over the years many folks have asked "how did you come up with that?" I thank all of them for being part of the inspiration for this book.

Most of all, however, I thank my students for all they have taught me. Over the years, we have performed some amazing shows and created that "magic" on stage. In the end, it's the ACTING that I'll remember most. I tell my students that each production is like a piece of cake. You can have a piece of cake in front of you that is decorated so beautifully, but if it tastes lousy when you bite into it, that's what you'll remember. While the sets and the props are like the fancy icing and sprinkles, the actors are the cake. It doesn't matter how elaborate the sets are – if the acting is lousy, the audience won't enjoy the performance. Over time I've learned to appreciate that simple sets are all you need – just like cake with a basic buttercream frosting. I dedicate this book to all who helped to build the sets and props within this book. Thanks for the many hours you gave in taking a bunch of cardboard and duct tape and helping to bring so many of my crazy ideas to life!

Chapter One
THE SET BUILDING TOOL KIT

I remember the first show I ever directed and produced. I had thirteen actors from ages 7-13 and we were performing an adaptation of *The Wizard of Oz*. I had a working budget of approximately $200 for everything and no clue where to start. I made some mistakes that year, and learned what did and didn't work. And I began to assemble my "set building tool kit" which I reuse yearly for the absolute basics. A 24 qt. clear bin with latch handles helps you to locate items quickly. A basic set building tool kit should contain the following:

- a hammer
- at least two screwdrivers – one flat head and one Philips head (having four is better – each one in two different sizes)
- 1-2 box cutters (get those with retractable blades for safety)
- measuring tape (at least 6 ft. / longer is better)
- ruler (I prefer the plastic ones that you can see through)
- pencils
- scissors (at least two pair if you have others helping you)
- level
- sharpies (several in various tip points and colors)

- stapler
- duct tape (I tried to have gray, white, and black as standard) (duct tape also comes in LOTS of designer colors and patterns)
- Gorilla tape (like duct tape but a bit stronger – for bigger jobs)
- scotch tape (I buy the rolls in bulk / dispensers are optional
- masking tape
- small container of nails, hooks, and clips
- string
- container with glue gun and supply of glue sticks

While specific items vary with each production, there are the basics that you'll use almost every time. The set bin does NOT have items like cordless drills, circular saws, or even staple guns. Those things can be useful, as you may need them for certain individual set pieces. However, this book is designed to show you how to build sets WITHOUT needing those items.

As for cost, a lot of these items can be found around your house. During the early years, I literally raided our home tool kit and returned items after the performance. Over time, though, I've built up permanent items from cast donations or gradual purchases.

The biggest expense of the tool kit each year is the tape. As a general rule, I might have a MINIMUM of 3-4 rolls of duct tape each year and another 5-6 rolls of scotch tape (transparent, not shiny!). I usually only keep one roll of Gorilla tape in the kit as I only use that when I need extra strength for an item, or it has to stay up for a longer period of time. I use masking tape mostly to mark floors for scene changes, so 1-2 rolls is sufficient. Since tape can be a bit expensive, I try to watch for sales and purchase rolls intermittently throughout the year in order to have what I need when show time arrives.

So now that the tool kit is assembled, what the heck do I do with it?

Chapter Two
SET TERMINOLOGY

Before you begin building a set, it's important as a director that you understand some of the basic theatre terminology. If you will be working with students and helping them grow as actors, it's vital to not only teach them the craft of acting, but also to increase their knowledge of their environment. Years down the road, a future director will say a quiet "thank you" to you for teaching students about what things are called and where they are located.

While every stage might be different, there are some basic terms that all directors should know. This chapter will cover the basics in labeling the stage and area around it. Diagram 2.1 shows a basic stage – assume you are looking at it from the audience. It's set up like a tic-tac-toe board, with nine distinct places where actors can be. When you begin working with new actors, be sure they understand the various places. It's also important to remember that as a director sitting in the audience, stage directions are from the perspective of the ACTOR ON STAGE, and not from where you are sitting. (For example, if you want someone to cross the stage to "stage left", he will actually move toward YOUR right).

Beyond actual stage directions, the stage has a number of other terms that every director should know. You may never work in an environment where all of these items are present, but you should at least know what they are. Diagram 2.2 labels the basic parts of a stage.

Diagram 2.1

upstage right (USR)	upstage center (USC)	upstage left (USL)
center stage right (CSR)	center stage (CS)	center stage left (CSL)
down stage right (DSR)	down stage center (DSC)	down stage left (DSL)

(audience / director)

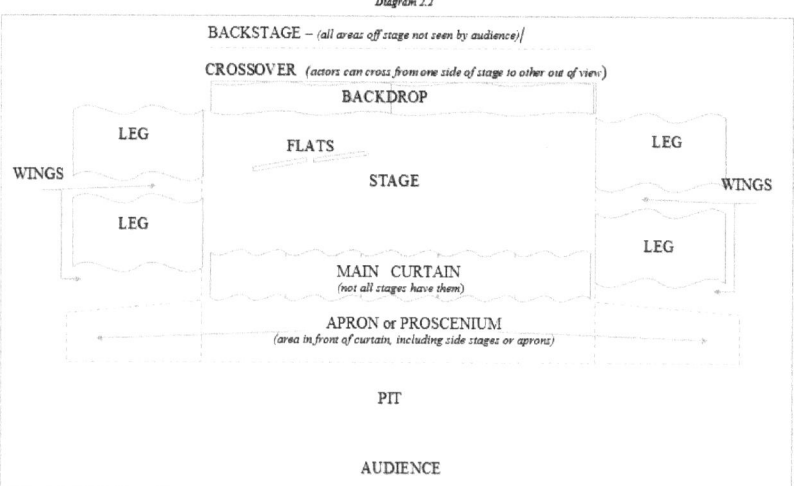

Diagram 2.2

BACKSTAGE – *(all areas off stage not seen by audience)*

CROSSOVER *(actors can cross from one side of stage to other out of view)*

BACKDROP

LEG   FLATS   LEG

WINGS   STAGE   WINGS

LEG   LEG

MAIN CURTAIN
(not all stages have them)

APRON or PROSCENIUM
(area in front of curtain, including side stages or aprons)

PIT

AUDIENCE

You might have an elaborate space complete with backstage areas, side wings, and actual curtains and legs, or a much simpler stage. A "black box" theatre is a simple room with a bare performance area. Sometimes the walls are actually painted black. If you are working in a classroom, a gym, or on a simple raised stage with no curtains, you are basically working within a "black box" setting. You may have no main curtain, and no back curtain. You most likely don't have "wing" space. Sometimes you might even be out in the open with audience wrapped around the performing space. Learning to build simple sets is especially vital in creating believable settings on the barest of stages.

There are a few key terms that will be used more than others in this book:

BACKDROP – usually stationary along the back / can be wood, cloth, or the wall

FLAT - can be stationary or mobile; used once or repeatedly to create a setting for specific scenes

STANDEE - freestanding piece of scenery that is easily moved on and off stage

SCENE CHANGE - the movement of various set pieces in between scenes to create a new setting

STRIKE A SET - at the end of the production, the set is taken down and put away

BLOCKING - the directions given to an actor on where to move about the stage

. . .

PROP - Any item an actor might carry on to use during a scene. The actor might carry the item on, or it might be set in place by someone else.

COSTUME - What the actor is wearing while on stage.

In some of the sets I've created, I've used flats as a stationary backdrop. In other words, once they are in position, they don't move for the entire show. However, their actual construction might be the same as other moving flats.

In my current location, I hang a black curtain as a backdrop to offer actors a backstage area with a crossover, and then use moving flats to create the scenery. As the scenes change, the flats are repositioned or rotated to create new settings. Keeping a SIMPLE overall set design helps to determine what types of flats work best and how many you need.

Chapter Three
BASIC SET DESIGN

The set designer is the person who designs and creates what the stage will look like for a production. In more professional theater settings the set designer will work with the director and a team of individuals to construct the set. If you are working in a children's theatre setting or in a classroom, chances are you ARE the set designer – and quite often, you are the one constructing the set as well.

When you have a limited budget and a basic space, the key is simplicity. The process follows these steps:

1. Read through your script, jotting down where each scene takes place
2. Determine the overall setting of the piece. Does the story take place in a certain time frame? Will you keep it there, or change it? (For example, the play *Much Ado About Nothing* by William Shakespeare was originally written in 1600, and set in Messina. One adaptation might be to move it to the mid 1940's and change the setting to someplace in the US. The STORY might not change, but how you design the set might be altered quite a lot.
3. Look at your list of scenes and determine which ones need

the most space. Any scenes with full cast or with dance numbers will need to have plenty of open space to move about. Smaller scenes might be played on the side aprons or in front of the main acting space using just props, seating, or standees to convey a different place.
4. Establish how many "places" you need to create. Once you have a firm understanding of where each scene takes place, you can begin to visual the various pieces that will be assembled to create your overall set design.
5. Plan where you need entrances and exits on stage. Note that actual DOORS are not vital to go in and out of a scene. An offstage door with a "knock" or bell costs nothing and still conveys entrances and exits. You also might be able to use aisles for entrances and exits if there is access for actors to reach them. This choice engages the audience and keeps their focus if you can utilize it.

Once you have a visual idea on what your basic set will look like, being able to show others your visual plan is imperative. Whether you sketch it out on scrap paper, create it in 3D form with cardstock and paper, or design it on a computer, a set designer (if you have one) needs to be able to "see" what's inside your head. In addition, your CAST benefits from seeing what your design is, as it gives them a sense of what their settings will look like. This is important in earlier blocking rehearsals as they'll have a mental image of where walls and other set pieces might be on the stage. Finally, those that might assist you in assembling the set will appreciate having a visual aide of some kind in front of them. Knowing that all cast and crew can understand your visual plan will help throughout the production process.

To illustrate, here's a simple set design showing two farm scenes and a fair scene. In diagram 3.1, you'll see a simple outdoor farm scene made with portable flats (more on that in chapter 4). In diagram 3.2, you'll see the same flats turned around to show another scene on the farm. Finally, diagram 3.3 shows a fair scene made by using the same flats from diagram 3.1 and adding a paper or cardboard carnival sign. The "wooden" fences are also just made of cardboard and lean against the black curtain. Three separate locations can easily be created using a minimum of materials and expenses.

Diagram 3.1 – Farm # 1

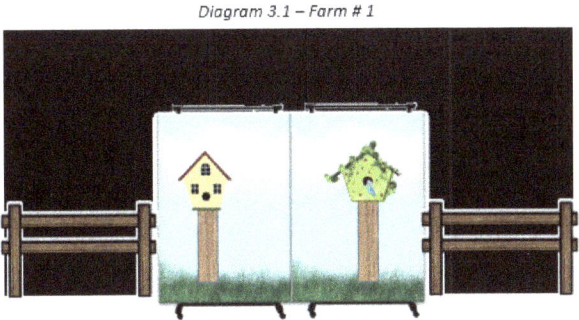

Diagram 3.2 – Farm # 2

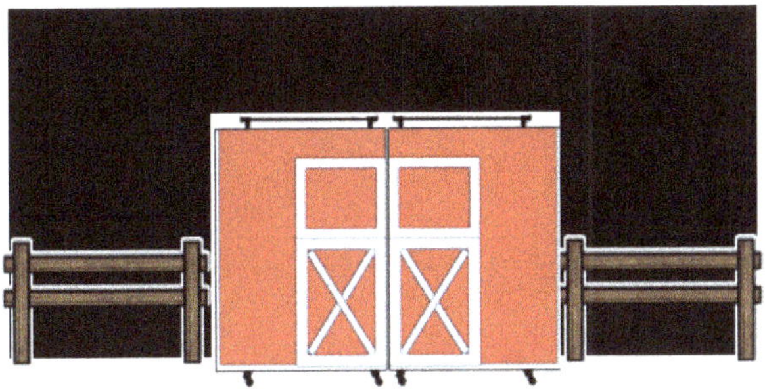

Diagram 3.3 – Fair scenes

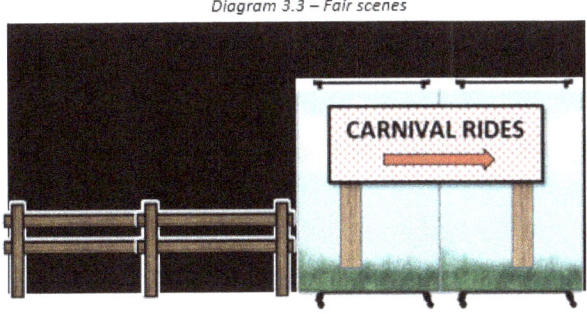

Diagram 3.4 shows an overall set design used for the inside of a home. Even though many walls and doors are missing, distinct places are defined on the stage: the lower level is the living room, and the upper level is a bedroom for the children. There are no doors, but cast members enter from the "outside" downstage right by the fireplace. The exit downstage left by the piano leads to the "kitchen". Upstage right there is another "hallway" exit behind the blue flat. Once cast members see the overall plan, they learn their blocking patterns to avoid walking through the blue walls that are built closer to performance time.

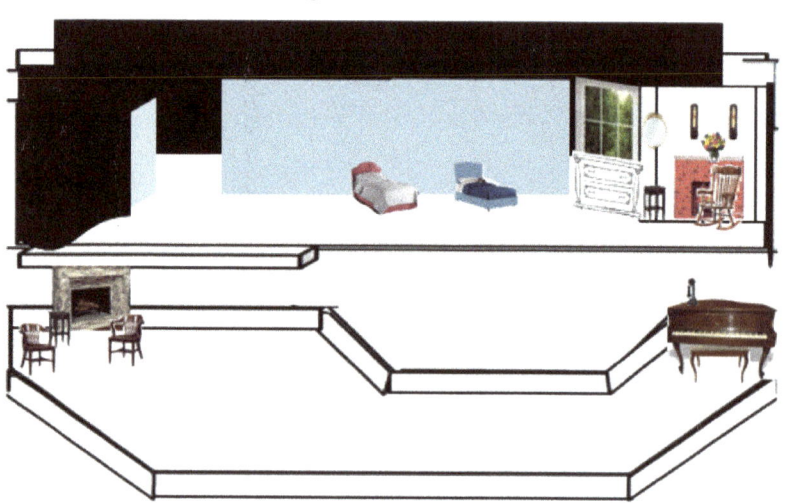

Diagram 3.4 — Inside home

It's possible to utilize various set pieces for more than one setting in the production. While an elaborate budget would allow for more authentic "period" pieces, it's not a necessity to make the setting believable to the audience. You will find that a small collection of set and furniture pieces can be used again and again in a variety of ways.

This is a list of some basic set pieces that have great versatility:

- **small table(s)** -- the round ones with three legs that screw in are lightweight and easy to carry, but can't support a lot of weight. They can be bare in a stark setting, and fancy with a tablecloth thrown over them. Folding card tables offer a bigger table when needed and are easy to move and store. Again, covered with a tablecloth, they can work for a variety of settings. You can also wrap colored paper around the legs or paint them if you don't want the "metal" look.

- **chairs / stools / crates** -- while almost any setting you perform in might have chairs that you can use, having a few pieces in your collection is handy. If storage is an issue, you can use metal folding chairs or plastic stacking chairs. The plain wooden straight backed chairs (like old school house chairs) work in a variety of settings and can be stacked by tipping the top chair over onto the bottom one. Having one upholstered chair for a fancier setting is a bonus, but not imperative. Always consider that any larger pieces have to be picked up, delivered, stored, and returned from where they are borrowed from, and a wooden chair can be easily draped with fabric for a lot less hassle. Stools are GREAT items that be used for both seating and small tables throughout your production. Finally, milk crates are easy to cover, can be sat on, stepped on, and provide storage inside while not in use. I always have a couple on hand!

- **old school desks** – the brown ones with the storage shelf inside can be used as desks, small tables, or covered with cardboard and decorated to look like bureaus, stone walls, and countless other items. They are usually also sturdy enough to be weight bearing so that a cast member could stand or sit on it. You can often find these at yard sales or thrift stores at a very reasonable price.

- **ottomans** –These are "investment" pieces, as they do cost a little bit, but the foldable ones with the removable cushioned tops are so versatile and equally easy to store that they are well worth the money. On sale they cost between $30-40 each, but having a couple in your inventory will allow you to use them for beds, benches, window seats, couches, and more. Each supports over 200 pounds in weight and they hold up extremely well over time.

- **wooden shelf** – Having a small portable unit with shelf space is SO useful. Whether being used for a kitchen unit to hold plates and pantry items, a school unit to hold books and classroom supplies, or another indoor setting, having a small portable piece with storage is always handy.

- **rolling cart (s)** – This is either another investment piece or a piece to try and borrow from time to time. You can find smaller wire carts for around $20, or slightly more sturdy utility carts for $50-70. The latter might be more economical to borrow, but you might not have as much flexibility for decorating or rehearsing. Rolling carts help to create another whole setting by just rolling them on and off stage. For example, they were used in a recent production to create a department store, with each one portraying a separate department (e.g. watches/jewelry, stationary/gifts, perfume/make up, and toys). In another production, they were used as various machines in a factory, and in yet another production they were used a candy store and a bookseller's store.

Some of these pieces can be found at no cost, or perhaps donated by people you know who don't need them anymore. Some you might have in your home already. The key is to look for simple items that can be used over and over again. Sets really CAN be created on a shoestring budget with some flexibility and creativity!

Chapter Four
FLAT BUILDING WITH CARDBOARD

When I was starting my directing career cardboard was almost an obsession. My daughters and I would be driving along when all of a sudden I'd stop the car, yell "cardboard!", and then get out and rescue big pieces from trash piles, parking lot dumpsters, and cornfields. Eventually I learned you could walk into places like furniture warehouses and be given all the free cardboard you could haul. I also discovered some resources for buying cardboard pieces that were reasonably priced and NEW (see appendix B).

As for decorating them, I initially painted the cardboard directly; later on I discovered how reasonably priced rolls of colored and patterned paper were, and that they could be removed and rolled up to use again. It was this combination of 8-10 pieces of cardboard and patterned paper that ended up being quite cost effective over time.

There are many different ways to create your flats with cardboard, and the latter comes in ALL different sizes. The standard sized flat is 4' x 8', but because of their size, they often need a wooden frame to provide the needed support. This can be expensive when you add up the costs of lumber and tools, and the flats are often difficult to move around. Because I have spent most of my time working with children and young adults, I didn't need an 8' high flat; a 5'or 6' flat worked just as well and was cheaper. In addition, the smaller sized flats proved easier to move on stage and more efficient to store between productions.

The first two flat designs to follow are truly just cardboard and duct tape. That's all you need aside from paint or paper to cover your flats. These can be really easy to move, but maybe not as durable as flats that are mounted to a frame. You can make either a three sided unit or a four sided unit. Each side would provide a different scenery setting, and the units are rotated as needed for the current scene. Depending on how big your stage is, you might need three or four units to cover the space. For example, if you wanted a twelve foot backdrop, you'd need three or four units depending on whether your cardboard is three or four feet wide. Each unit would need three or four pieces of cardboard, resulting in a total of twelve to sixteen pieces for the space.

To build a three piece unit you need to know what three settings you want to portray. In the example below, there is an outdoor setting, an indoor setting that could be used as a house, a shop, a café, or any number of other places, and a brick wall – which again could be used as both indoor and outdoor settings.

To assemble, you can either paint/cover the cardboard FIRST, and then tape the unit together, or you can tape it together first and then cover each side (though this will require a place to store the units if they are not remaining on your stage). Also, when I didn't get to prepare the set and staging area until the day before a performance the assembly would HAVE to wait until I reached the venue.

Determine which setting will be numbers 1, 2, & 3 (note: you do NOT actually put the number on the flat – it's just an organizational tool to keep track of what order they should be in). Diagram 4.1 shows how you would assemble a three piece unit, folding the two sides around to meet in the back, forming a triangular shaped unit. You would tape the three edges where they meet on the sides of each piece.

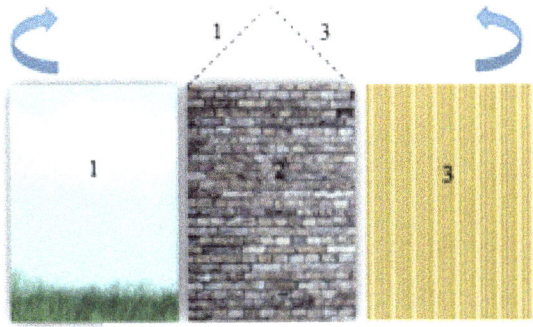

Diagram 4.1

You'd repeat the same process for how many units you'd want crossing the stage. For example, using cardboard pieces that are 40 x 60 (my preferred size to work with), three units side by side would give you 120 inches, which is ten feet. One more added and you'd have over thirteen feet. Using the same designs as above, you would assemble each unit in the same manner, and then line them up with sides touching for whatever scene you are using. The view from the front would look like this (diagram 4.2):

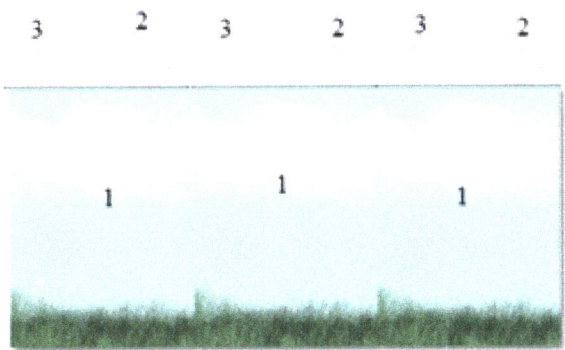

Diagram 4.2

From the back the set up would look like this (diagram 4.3):

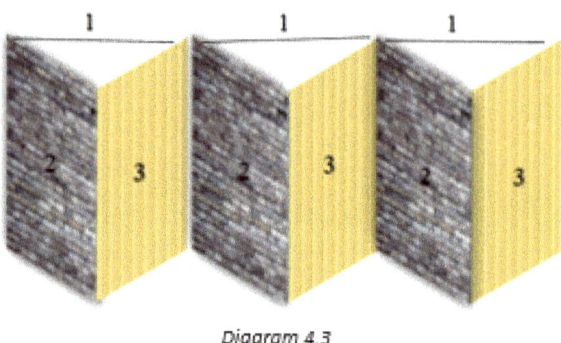

Diagram 4.3

When the scene changes to the next setting, the units are all rotated in the same direction. The next two settings would then look like this (diagram 4.4):

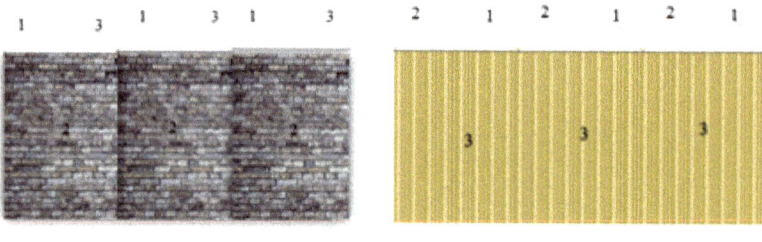

Diagram 4.4

For each of the units, other simple changes can be made by hanging something from the top or leaning something against it. (Note; keep in mind when JUST using cardboard, you can't hang anything too heavy from the top or the weight of it might cause the unit to fall over.)

In this illustration (diagram 4.5), another piece of cardboard is brought out and leaned against the triangular unit to create a witch's cauldron and fireplace in a castle. In the second illustration, adding a framed "picture" makes the setting look more like a home or office. The easiest way to hang things from the top is using a simple binder clip on the top of the unit. Lightweight string or ribbon will hang quite easily by hooking it around the top of the clip.

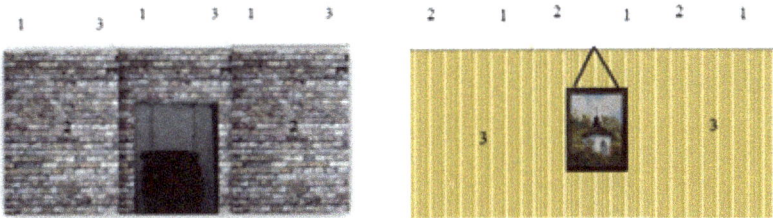

Diagram 4.5

If you decided that you really needed a fourth separate setting that couldn't be adapted from the others or played without a backdrop, you could try a FOUR sided unit. Refrigerator boxes are perfect for this; however, many appliance manufacturers now wrap them in bubble wrap instead, so finding an assembled box might not be easy.

You can still create your own using the same directions for the three sided unit except you'll have an extra side, and from the back the "box" units will have a complete setting showing as well. They key is to make sure the scenery shots are in the same order all around the unit, as shown in diagram 4.6. In the bottom illustration, the grass/sky scene would show along the back of the units when the wallpaper scene was showing on stage.

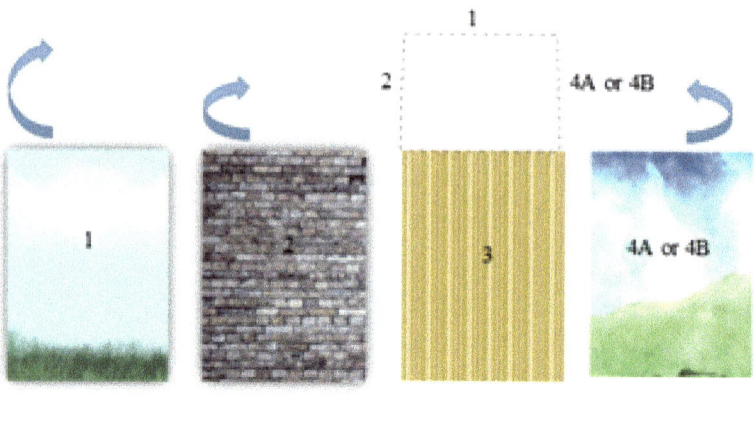

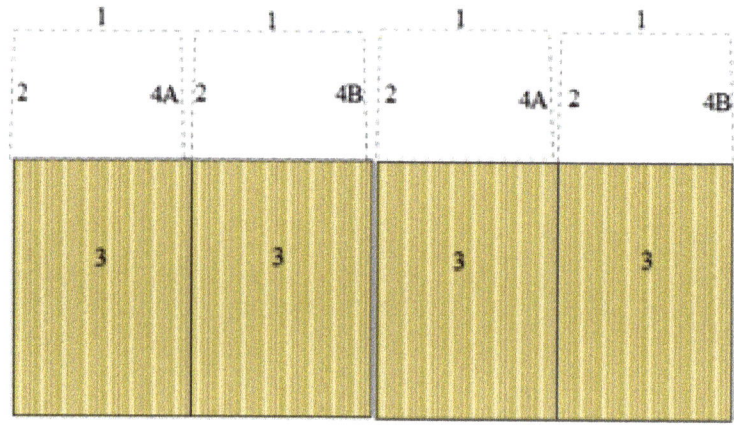

Diagram 4.6

If you wanted to have a little more variety with a particular piece of scenery, you can do so – the secret is to make sure you keep the pieces in order on all the units, and figure out the correct order for the assembled units so that the varied scenery lines up correctly when seen. When starting to assemble, it's wise to start with the varied scenery first. In this set up, the "castle/brick wall" scene would be visible along the back on the four units.

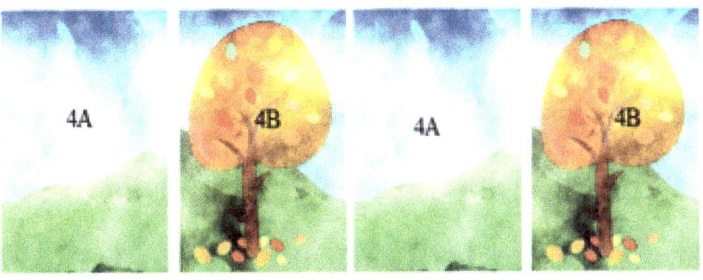

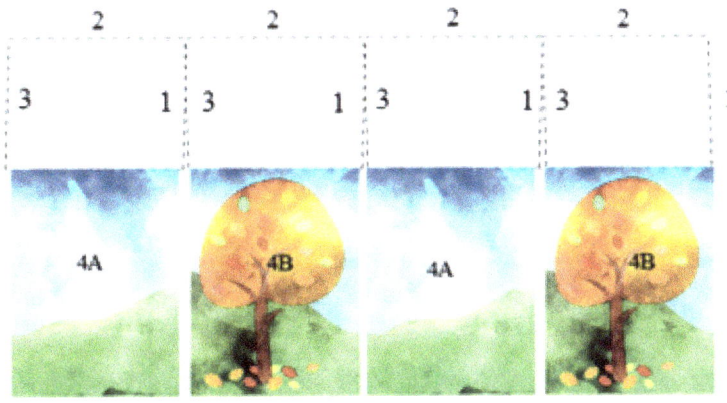

Diagram 4.7

While the free standing cardboard units are easy to make and rotate, I prefer something a little more durable while remaining easy to move around the stage. As stated earlier, the standard 4' x 8' flats were more expensive, harder to move, and bulkier to store. Because my productions tended to be for a younger cast, I decided that the higher flats were both too expensive and too hard for younger kids to move during scene changes. The answer for me was to use shorter flats on a lighter frame that was easier to assemble and move.

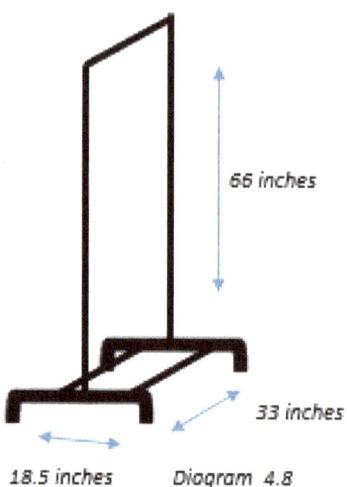

Diagram 4.8

My solution did require a small investment for the racks, but they can be used over and over and are easy to assemble and strike down. The "racks" are portable costume racks (diagram 4.8) that can be found online or in any major department store. I paid $15.00 for each and have four (when not using all of them for the backdrop, you can also use one for costumes backstage). These portable racks also allow different heights. If you want a shorter flat, you just adjust while assembling. Assembly only takes about fifteen minutes. Using a flat with a 60" height, the cardboard sits on the bottom bars and comes up just under the bottom of the top bar.

The cardboard size that I attach to them is usually around 40" x 60". Again, they come up almost to the top of the rack frame and stick out on either side to allow taping the two flats together. If you use the 40" x 60" with three racks, your backdrop will be ten feet across. Add the fourth rack and you'll have just about 13 ½ feet.

You can purchase these sheets relatively inexpensively, either through a office supply catalog or online – please note that if you are having them delivered you might pay twice the amount of the cardboard to have them arrive. If there are places where you can go and pick them up, it will save you lots of money – you just need a vehicle large enough to hold them. (Any van or SUV will work). Another option is to check out moving stores and office supply stores for unassembled boxes. Cutting them in half or taping two together might be cheaper. You can also try places like furniture stores or warehouses for bigger boxes and ask for them to be set aside for you.

To assemble, you first put together the racks; there are no tools required for assembly on these, and they are remarkably stable as long as they are put together straight. Directions for assembly are included in the box; as you work, just be sure that the vertical and horizontal pieces are perpendicular. If they are not, the rack will either look a little warped, tip to one side, or show one wheel not entirely on the ground. Just adjusting the various bars by turning them a bit will solve this problem.

The next step is to prepare each piece of cardboard. Some choose to paint; if you choose this option, you'll need to buy more cardboard for each production unless you paint "generic" scenes that can used in various shows. If you can afford another small investment, purchasing rolls of patterned and plain paper will give you authentic looking sets and a supply that should last for several shows. Most rolls contain 25 feet of design, and can be under $20 each. If that option is still higher than your budget allows, or if you don't have a budget, you can also find various rolls of wrapping paper at dollar and discount stores than can be just as effective; usually two rolls from a dollar store will cover a flat.

To cover the cardboard, you can cut it to the exact size so that the edges will line up flush with the cardboard edges. Because cast members can catch an edge with their finger when going to move the flats in between scenes, allow for a couple of inches around the sides so you can fold it around to the back and then fasten it with duct tape. This latter option gives the edges a much cleaner look, and the paper is more secure on the cardboard. Once the production is over, you can carefully detach the paper from the cardboard after the show, remove the tape (or fold it over so no "sticky" sides are still found), roll it up, and store it away for a future production, knowing it's already cut and ready to attach.

Once your cardboard pieces are painted or covered, you're ready to assemble the flats. It's easier to complete this task with the help of another person, as one can hold the cardboard while the other tapes, but it's not hard to complete alone. If working by yourself, get the cardboard in place, have a few pieces of duct tape already cut, and hold the cardboard with one hand while taping with the other. Once you get a couple of pieces to "hold" it, you can then continue without it falling over. Starting with one piece of cardboard, you place it on the rack (with scenery side facing AWAY from the rack) with the bottom edge on the rack right up against the center poles. The top of the flat should come to within an inch or two of the top bar. Make sure the piece is centered so that you have equal space on each side of the center pole. Tape the back of the cardboard onto the rack pole as shown below (diagram 4.9), Taping the cardboard to the top bar is optional (as shown on the right), but it does give a little extra support and covers the gap a bit. This first piece should be firmly attached to the rack.

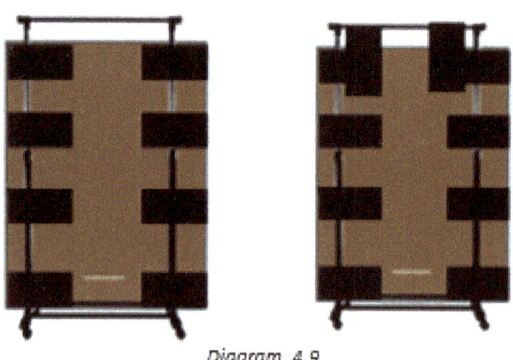

Diagram 4.9

Once the first piece of cardboard is secure, take the second piece and place it on the rack with the scenery facing outward, and again line up the bottom edge close to the center pole. Positioning this piece is easier as you can line up the edges with the cardboard that is already attached. Note with this piece that you can't easily tape it on the BACK as there's only a couple of inches to work with between the flats. To attach to the POLE, you can tape a couple of small pieces along the top edge where the poles meet at the corner, or up and over the bar a bit. However, most of the taping will be a few strategically placed pieces along the side edges. The duct tape should be long enough to start on the FRONT of one flat and cross over the gap between the sides to attach to the front of the other flat. Keep in mind that you don't want to have it TOO long, as the ends are visible on the front of each.

As shown in the illustration below (diagram 4.10), the color of duct tape is an important choice. For each design, you'll see on the left flat that black tape was used to show the placement of the tape; on the right flat, a lighter color was used, which was much less prominent on the finished flat. When designing your set, keep in mind what color duct tape works best for each flat assembly. Once flats are assembled, you now have a basic backdrop that can be moved, rotated, and adjusted as needed. Now let's move on to actually using them to create a wide variety of settings!

Diagram 4.10

INDOOR SETTINGS

No matter what show or play you are directing, there are various types of settings used. The focus of the scene should determine the vital set pieces, and then just add one or two smaller items to create the mood. Another aspect that helps create setting is lighting and sound, which is discussed in a later chapter. The indoor settings in this chapter are generic so that they can be utilized in a variety of productions. Indoor settings include:

Parts of a house -

- living rooms
- dining rooms
- kitchens
- bedrooms / nurseries
- attics / basements

Places for work and learning -

- schoolrooms
- offices and factories

Places for eating –

- restaurants
- bars / taverns / pubs
- cafes

Parts of a castle –

- ballrooms
- throne rooms
- dungeons
- towers

Other public meeting places –

- libraries
- department stores / malls
- town halls / gymnasiums
- movie theaters
- churches
- bus / train stations
- sporting arenas

INDOOR SPACES - LIVING ROOMS:

Most people, when thinking of living rooms, imagine soft, comfy couches with pillows, big flat screen TVs, and various chairs, tables, lamps, and shelves. However, if you are on a shoestring budget, many of these items are both expensive and hard to move both on and off the stage. If you have access to a couch or love seat and the manpower to move it, it's not a bad thing to include, but in reality living rooms are gathering places – a place where people can sit and talk and spend time. Even without the couch, there may be other ways to show the space.

The easiest solution if you have no couch is to use several chairs put together and covered with a sheet or blanket; add a couple of pillows and a small table, and it's functional.

Another "couch" option, if you should have the ottomans discussed earlier, is to put them lengthwise together, and either cover them or leave them as is. Put up against a flat with a pillow or two, it conveys the main seating area nicely. Add a couple of stools with cloth napkins or fabric covering and a small vase with flowers and you have a lovely "living" room, as seen here in diagram 5.1.

Diagram 5.1

One creative option I used recently was stacking two big gymnastics mats together and covering them with a blanket and pillow. Anyone who rehearses in a dance studio or school gym might choose to use this option if mats are available. Another gymnastic mat stood behind the first with another cloth covering that served as a multi-purpose "table." Although the couch had no back, it easily held three of my actors and visually helped to create the space. See diagram 5.2 for the photo of this living room set.

Diagram 5.2

INDOOR SPACES - DINING ROOMS:

Unless you are doing a show where the dining room is a key setting in the plot (such as a production of *Clue*), a dining room is rarely necessary in children's theater. It can easily be incorporated into a living room set with a table off to one side with entrances and exits from that side of the stage to the offstage kitchen. Any food or dishes can easily be carried in from that side for scenes with eating, but then you still have a table and chairs for other scenes that might take place in the living room.

The key for portraying a dining room is *simplicity*. Try never to have more chairs than is necessary in any given scene. Even if there are four or five people in a scene, unless they are all seated to eat, you might not need more than three chairs, as the cast members might be standing or moving back and forth from the offstage "kitchen" with food.

For a production of *Arsenic and Old Lace*, a simple card table was used with three chairs, leaving the downstage edge of the table open. A lace tablecloth covered the table and a smaller table with shelving was off to the side as a hutch to hold plates, cups, two battery operated candles, a tea tray, and a few canisters of wine. On the table sat only a small vase with silk flowers (see diagram 5.3). Any food was offstage and brought in and out. Since the play is set entirely in the living / dining area of the house, this part of the set was vital – however, it was both simple and effective use of space.

Diagram 5.3

INDOOR SPACES - KITCHENS:

Like the dining room, a kitchen should be kept as simple as possible. One key factor in designing a kitchen is the *time period* of the production; for example, a kitchen from *Fiddler on the Roof* will look much different than a kitchen from *Bye Bye Birdie*. However, they can still be kept minimal. Another key factor in designing your kitchen is determining what actions are in the script that need certain parts of the kitchen to be present. In *Bye Bye Birdie*, for example, there is a scene where Mae Peterson kneels down to stick her head in the oven; obviously, some image of an oven with a door that opens should be present. In *Fiddler*, however, there is no need to have an oven that opens. A three dimensional oven might be nothing more than a cardboard box painted, or a piece of cardboard wrapped around a small desk or table. Even simpler, a TWO dimensional image of a stove might be attached to the flat.

Again, the *action* in the setting is important to know as you plan. A kitchen is generally a place where food preparation is being done, or food is being eaten. It can be as simple as a table with a couple of chairs and a place to have props to one side – whether a shelving unit, a cardboard box painted to look like a cabinet unit, or a portable cabinet that's easy to move on and off. Having an actual refrigerator, sink, and oven is not usually needed for children's theatre productions.

One item that a kitchen usually has is a *window* of some kind. This can be attached to your flat, and if you want to add a little three dimensional effect, you can add curtains. There are websites where you can download free images of all kinds of windows (both indoor and outdoor). You can then print them and attach them for a realistic look. See diagram 5.4 for a simple kitchen set.

Diagram 5.4

INDOOR SPACES - BEDROOMS / NURSERIES:

Bedrooms can be a challenge to create on stage – especially in children's theatre – as beds tend to be large and bulky. Any scene changes become more difficult, partly due to the size of the set piece being moved, as well as where to PUT them off stage. Many venues do not allow a lot of room backstage for large set pieces or places to store your set pieces between rehearsals. If you are using a space that you only have access to for a short time, it means that you will be moving ALL of your set pieces back and forth within a day or two of the performance. Bigger set pieces make this process more arduous.

There are still a couple of ways to create sleeping spaces. If you need to have a bed that will be sat on, slept in, and even stood on, you can either build a smaller sized bed that a child can still fit in, or create one using some of your "key" set pieces. For example, if you are in that space with gym mats, they could be stacked up with a bedspread and pillow over it and you've got almost a full sized bed that functions well and moves relatively easily.

If you have the ottomans as part of your inventory, they can be attached to a couple of chairs to create a "short" bed. Once covered with bedding and pillow, there is a sturdy place to sit on the end of the bed, and a child can still curl up on the chairs under the bedding to "sleep" if needed. One note on assembling a bed this way; if attached with both duct tape and rope, they stay together well, but they are a little awkward to move. Placing the entire bed on a piece of cardboard might make it easier to slide on and off stage if needed. See diagrams 5.6 and 5.7 for construction and the final look.

Diagram 5.6

BED CONSTRUCTION –

- Take two blue chairs – duct tape inside legs together to form one "bench"
- Try putting either casters of a piece of cardboard under cloth ottoman for easier moving / sliding
- Tape or tie with rope ottoman to the chairs to make one single piece
- Cut out cardboard "headboard" and attach to front of chair
- Cover entire piece with bedding – tech person should be able to hide behind to pull covers up with fishing line attached

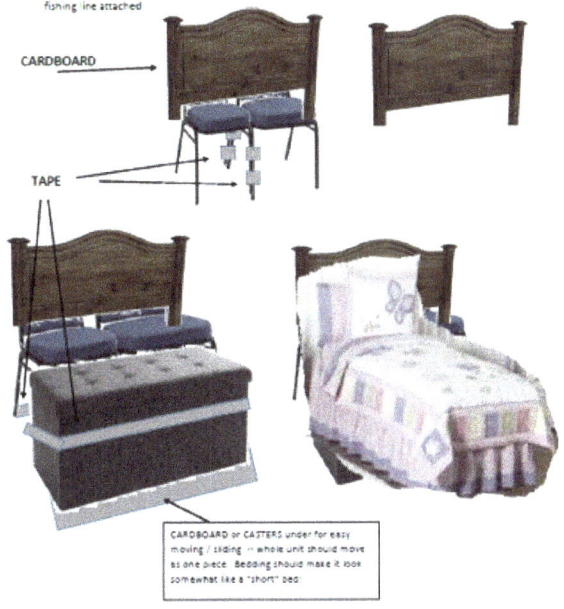

CARDBOARD

TAPE

CARDBOARD or CASTERS under for easy moving / sliding – whole unit should move as one piece. Bedding should make it look somewhat like a "short" bed.

Diagram 5.7

To make a "bureau" that doesn't need to open, use a piece of cardboard taped around a small table or desk. The one below was made in this manner with dollar store wrapping paper attached to the cardboard. A big black sharpie was used to draw the knobs and drawers. From the audience it looked just like a white wooden bureau.

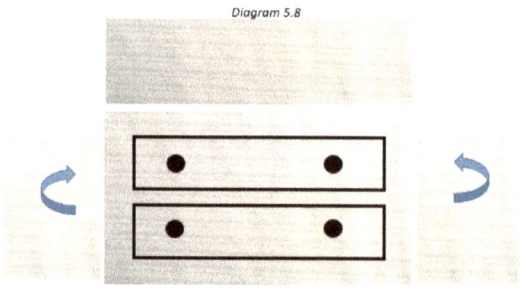

Diagram 5.8

Tape pieces together at corners of desk and fold side pieces back along sides of desk and top piece onto top of desk -- Use marker to sketch the drawers and knobs

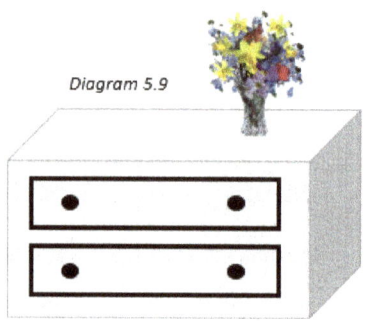

Diagram 5.9

Depending on your production, a bedroom or nursery shouldn't need much more than a place to sleep and a place to put clothes. There are a few variations that might involve just one or two simple adjustments. For a nursery, it might be as simple as a rocking chair and a cradle which can either be carried on and off to create the scene in front of other sets, or placed off on a side apron.

If it's necessary for a woman to "primp" in front of a mirror, one can be made with a cardboard border and shiny mylar paper for the glass on the wall. Another option is a three dimensional mirror that she sits behind but the audience sees her face through the frame. The mirror frame can be painted cardboard that is attached to a small desk skirted with fabric on the downstage side. The top of the desk could hold just a tray with assorted make up and beauty items, along with a hair brush or comb. With a little extra expense, you could fasten some battery operated Christmas lights around the frame to make it look like a fancy makeup mirror.

INDOOR SPACES - ATTICS / BASEMENTS:

Both attics and basements tend to be places that we go to for a specific purpose, such as to find something, or explore. They often create an aura of mystery or nostalgia. If a character might sleep in the attic – like in *Cinderella* and *A Little Princess*-- treat it more like a bedroom with adjustments.

If the space IS just an attic or basement, use a side apron or a place in front of the other set and add a few set pieces such as an old trunk, cardboard boxes labeled with contents, and a few items than have been stored and forgotten (e. g. a dollhouse, ice skates, or a sewing mannequin).

INDOOR SPACES – PLACES FOR LEARNING AND WORKING:

School rooms rarely require a separate desk and chair for every student. All you really need to convey a school room is to have kids sitting in either chairs or on benches, and a teacher's desk off to one side or in the middle. Add in a visual or two like a map on the flat or an apple on the desk, and the audience will get the idea. Even more important than the LOOK of the setting is the actions of the people in it. If a teacher is presenting a lesson, or students are reading or writing (or using tablets or slates depending on the time period), it will be very evident that school is in session. Consider a few chairs or benches toward the sides with the desk in the middle to open up a space for movement and interaction throughout the "classroom," especially if dance numbers are involved.

Offices and workspaces can also be conveyed without "desks" or "workstations" for every person. It might suffice to have just one or two for key actors, and then utilize the walls or flats/backdrops to complete the look. A desk or small table with a phone, a jar with pens and pencils, and a computer keyboard or typewriter is enough to show it's a work space. The same concept works in a "factory" – just one or two workstations on a small table with some empty stacked boxes and a calendar on the wall can create an "industrial" look.

See diagrams 5.10 and 5.11 that show how to use the same set piece to create a school room and a factory setting.

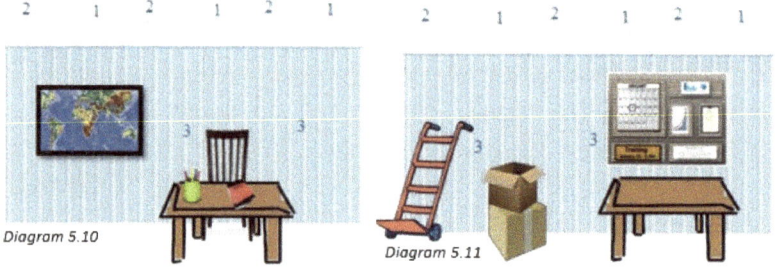

Diagram 5.10

Diagram 5.11

INDOOR SPACES – PLACES FOR EATING AND DRINKING:

Whether you are staging a restaurant, a café, or a pub, first consider how many cast members will be on stage. If this is a setting where there will be dancing, be sure to keep a large space open. Usually just two or three tables with two or three chairs at each is enough for any leads with major dialogue. Other cast members might sit on stools, benches, or stand about the space while chatting.

If you are in a fancier restaurant, the food station would not be present on stage. Waiters would enter and exit from an offstage kitchen and make their way around the space carrying trays to deliver and collect items. Tables might have small linen table cloths and a candle or flower in the middle. If the tables are smaller to give more open space, consider using salad or dessert sized plates. That way you can serve a couple of people without filling the tabletop.

For a tavern or 50s soda fountain, you might want a bar or food counter off to the side or you can place two rolling cards end to end to create a longer counter space. Cover the front and two sides with cardboard and "wood" grained paper, and then have the top for "counter space" and the shelf underneath for items such as plates, cups, rags, and food. You can do the same with any table or shelving unit; if it doesn't come with shelves underneath, you can bring out a milk crate or plastic bin to keep underneath for needed items. The key is to have everything easy to carry on and off if you have to move the set piece during the show. Add a couple of stools in front and you have room for a couple more cast members to sit and interact with someone behind the counter.

Here is a 50s diner set (diagram 5.12) with open space for dancing. The counter on the left had shelving underneath and a couple of stools for seating. Each table had three chairs to keep all cast visible. Other cast members gathered upstage center or off to the sides of the two tables. There was a cardboard jukebox leaning against the back flat upstage left.

Diagram 5.12

INDOOR SPACES – PLACES IN A CASTLE:
Backdrop flats for a castle setting are easy – either patterned paper with gray bricks or a marble design both make simple starting backgrounds whether your castle belongs to a witch or a royal family. Depending on the production, you might only need to portray one

place in the castle; if you need more than one, here are a few simple adjustments to create a ballroom, throne room, dungeon, and tower using the same backdrop throughout.

For a ballroom, get silky table runners at a dollar store and attach the top to a couple of dowels. Tape some string to the ends, and they can hung over the gray backdrop using the top bar of the rolling flats (or office clips along the top of the cardboard if using just that). Use bright colors such as royal blue and white or gold (diagram 5.13). Put a couple of chairs off to one side, add a royal "crest" (drawn on poster board) or a cardboard photo frame of a royal ancestor and it can also work as your throne room.

Diagram 5.13

Diagram 5.14

For the dungeon, use plain gray with nothing extra. If it's a witches dungeon, you might add the cauldron (again, drawn on a free standing piece of cardboard) as shown again here (diagram 5.14).

For a tower, all you need is a couple of "windows" to hang with either sky or treetops off in the distance. If the character is interacting with someone outside, they can speak offstage while looking down to create the illusion that they are up high. See diagram 5.15

Diagram 5.15

INDOOR SPACES – PUBLIC MEETING PLACES:

Most public meeting spaces in a production will involve a good number of cast members, so again think spacing and portable items around the stage. A few spots to be considered here are libraries, shopping areas (malls/dept. stores), and town halls/gymnasiums.

For all three, we'll use the same backdrop with a couple of free standing pieces or hanging items. We'll also utilize a rolling cart or small portable table for book shelves, shopping department counters (e.g. cosmetics or jewelry), and a "podium" for a town hall. Add a couple of benches or a couple of chairs in downstage corners and you are set.

Chapter Six
OUTDOOR SETTINGS

Outdoor settings might include:

- front porches
- city or village streets
- roads in the country
- parks
- gardens
- farms
- fairgrounds
- campgrounds
- jungle or the woods
- beach
- mountains

OUTDOOR SPACES - PORCHES:
    Porches are for sitting and talking. While having one that's attached to a "house" with an actual door is nice, it's not needed to create the setting. Porches are one of the easiest "portable" sets to

create, as all you really are a couple of chairs and perhaps a small table and a railing. The railing can be either an old metal one found in someone's garage, or a piece of painted cardboard that stands by itself. Actors can exit to one side or another as they come and go, the audience will figure out that the actors are on a porch by the dialogue and activity.

Here's a simple "porch" setting done with just a couple of chairs and a railing made from a piece of cardboard that's painted or covered with "wood" grain paper. To make it stand up, cut a few slits along the bottom and attach a perpendicular piece to keep it from falling over (like paper dolls are made). Tape the support pieces in the back to make it sturdier. See diagram 6.1 below.

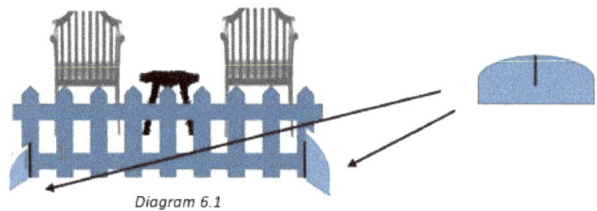

Diagram 6.1

Another option is to use one of the rolling costume racks (if you have an extra). When assembling, just use the two bottom side bars, and either attach the silver cross bar across the top or leave just the side bars alone, and then tape the cardboard railing to it……it will then move quite easily. See diagram 6.2.

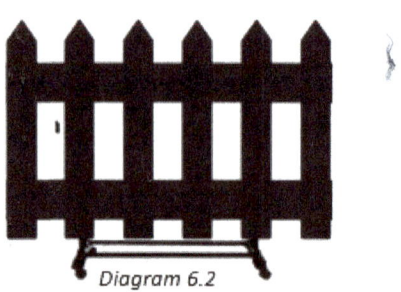

Diagram 6.2

OUTDOOR SPACES – CITY OR VILLAGE STREETS:

Outdoor streets can be played totally in front of another set if it's just one or two scenes. The dialogue and action will convey to the audience that they are not in the places set on stage, and if you should have lighting it's possible to darken the area behind to accent the scene further. However, some shows have a lot of action taking place outside, so needing outdoor sets is vital to the storyline.

The use of patterned paper or painted sets can turn cardboard in any number of buildings. Patterns can make the flat look like wood, brick, stone, or even marble. You can use one basic backdrop for all of the street scenes in one city such as London (see diagram 6.3). Various street merchants carried their "wares" with them in baskets. The bookseller had a wooden cart with books and a sign on it just "outside" an entrance. Various street sellers of the time included bread sellers, flower sellers, milk and dairy merchants, fruit sellers, and various "shoppers" who carried baskets to buy.

Photo 6.3

For outdoor settings that need to show more than one building, be sure to vary the look of the flats to help define each shop. If there are certain buildings that cast members have to "enter" and "exit," place those buildings at either end of the street and they enter by walking around behind it. Furthermore, the buildings don't have to be to "scale" in a children's production. Here's an example of Main Street in a small midwest town – cast members entered and exited between the library and telegraph office on one side, and the hotel and billiard parlor on the other. (see diagram 6.4)

This backdrop was visible for the entire show, with all other scenes being played down on the front thrust with just portable furniture and set pieces to establish the setting. Benches replaced the chairs for the actual production. Adding items like windows, lamp posts, and fake plants/trees helps to make the "outdoor" look more authentic.

Photo 6.4

OUTDOOR SPACES – PARKS AND GARDENS:

Outdoor scenes in parks and gardens can be extremely easy; starting with a plain blue flat, you can add grass, flowers, and trees in a couple of ways. One way is to lean a free standing piece of painted cardboard up against the blue flat. Another option is to tape another piece of patterned paper to the bottom section of the flat. You can also use fake plants and trees in front of it to finish the look. In diagram 6.5, wrapping paper with a floral pattern is taped at the bottom; in diagram 6.6, the tree is painted and cut out of cardboard and leaned against the flat which has been painted. If you don't have an artist to paint flowers, there are several online sites where you can download copyright free images; print them out in color and then either fasten them directly onto the background paper or mount them on cardboard and lean it against.

Diagram 6.5

Diagram 6.6

OUTDOOR SPACES – FARMS AND FAIRGROUNDS:

For a production of an adaptation of *Wizard of OZ*, I used the backdrop pictured in diagram 6.5 as the main "outdoor" flat for both the farm scene and Munchkin Land. In order to create more of a "farm" look, I utilized a couple of smaller set pieces on the sides. First, I placed my portable ottomans off to each side. I covered them with bath towels that were yellow-tan in color and then used some "hay" scrapbook paper taped to cardboard to make them look like hay bales. I used just four pieces for each, taped to two pieces of cardboard that were perpendicular to each other. The cardboard provided a little more stability so that they wouldn't fall off the ottoman and allowed a cast member to sit on them without ripping them. (see photo 6.7)

Behind the "hay bale" I used another small piece of cardboard with the flower wrapping paper, and then covered a portable ballet barre (you could also use a rolling costume rack at it's lowest height) into a split rail fence with a cornstalk at each end: (photo 6.8)

Photo 6.7

Photo 6.8

Other "farm" looks might include a red cardboard barn – this can be cut from cardboard and painted red or covered with red wrapping paper from the dollar store. The white markings can either be painted or cut out of white paper and attached. (diagram 6.9) Another easy thing to sketch onto cardboard and paint is a windmill cutout in black. (diagram 6.10)

Diagram 6.9

Diagram 6.10

OUTDOOR SPACES – CAMPGROUNDS AND THE WOODS (OR JUNGLE)

A campsite is an easy set to create with any outdoor backdrop; all you need is a tent and a little campfire. An actual tent should not be difficult to set up, but cardboard can certainly be used if one isn't available, and then the tent becomes part of the background. The campfire can be three dimensional or another cardboard cutout with a battery operated flame inside or behind it to create the campfire flame. The biggest challenge for a camping scene is the difference between day and night – if you have lighting available, a dimmer with some blue light creates a lovely nighttime scene. If that's not in the budget, then it's up to the actors to show the audience what time of day or night it is.

For the woods, any kind of fake and potted plants and trees are a huge help for some three dimensional set pieces. In addition to trees and greenery, you might have a stone wall along the way, a big rock, or even some spider webs. If bringing in lots of actual foliage is not practical, you can paint trees on cardboard with very little artistic talent (believe me, I am NOT an artist and have painted many!). Lighting again, if you have access to it, can be dimmed and given a green or blue tint. For the least amount of work, or if it's only one scene in your production, consider having the actors play the scene in front of other set pieces. Their actions and dialogue can convince the audience that the bushes and trees are behind them.

OUTDOOR SPACES -- MOUNTAINS AND THE BEACH:

Basic mountains are some of the easiest things to cut out of cardboard and paint – they can then be leaned against any backdrop with blue sky. If you are going to add any kind of building to the backdrop, be sure that the scale stays relative, or all of a sudden you'll have a good sized house that appears as big as the mountain next to it. Remember that if you don't have height to work with, then distance is the tool that creates a far away look. Your backdrop should appear to have far away objects on it.

If your scene takes you to the beach, you can use the plain blue backdrop and with beach towels and various props. A big beach umbrella adds color and dimension, but it's just as easy to create the setting with a pail and shovel, a container of sunscreen, and a colorful beach ball. A musical background track with ocean waves and seagulls would add even more credibility to the location. (diagram 6.11)

Diagram 6.11

Chapter Seven

MAGICAL / FANTASY SETTINGS

Magical settings might include:

- over the rainbow
- inside a mirror
- inside a painting
- under the sea
- North Pole / Santa's workshop
- animated or enchanted places with animals

MAGICAL/FANTASY SETTINGS– OVER THE RAINBOW

Most people think of the Land of Oz here, as there have been so many variations on the original story (e.g. *Wizard of Oz, Wicked, The Wiz*). Creating the various places in Oz doesn't require a full set change, however. Using a few key pieces with some colorful changes can be enough to change your settings. For example, the same backdrop can be used for the farm and Munchkin Land; if you add some bright colors and house with a pair of socks sticking out, you can easily transport Dorothy from Kansas to Oz. To create the Emerald City, add some green highlights. Here is a recent set showing the same backdrop being used for all three scenes (see diagrams 7.1, 7.2, and 7.3).

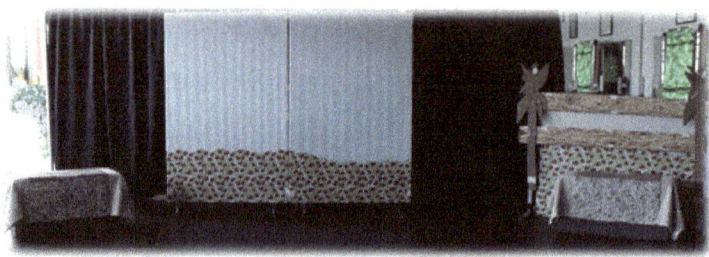

Diagram 7.1 - farm

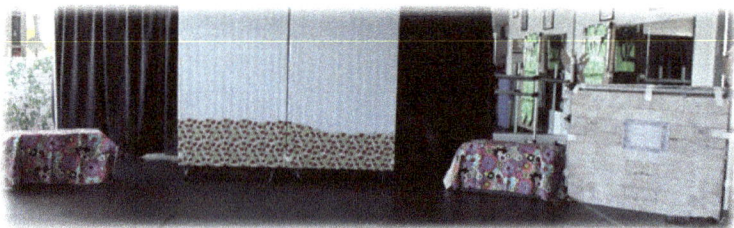

Diagram 7.2 Munchkinland

Diagram 7.3 – Emerald City

If you'd like to add an actual "yellow brick road," it can done with either cardboard painted yellow or a plastic tablecloth. Both can have "bricks" painted or drawn with sharpies. If using the tablecloth option, be sure that it is taped down well and be careful with your cast, as the plastic can be a little slippery. One more option is to have the yellow brick road travel out through the audience so that cast members can actually travel as scenes on stage are being changed (diagram 7.4).

Diagram 7.4

MAGICAL/FANTASY SETTINGS– INSIDE A MIRROR

Diagram 7.5

To allow the audience to SEE Alice or another character pass through the looking glass, use one of the rolling costume racks at full height. Two long pieces of shiny silver mylar paper taped to the rack with a big slit overlap in the middle actually does look like a mirror. One tip is to not place the mirror perpendicular to the audience as most lighting will just result in major glare off of the paper (see diagram 7.5). A painting could be done the same way, but would have to be painted on two pieces of paper to allow for the overlap hang in the middle.

. . .

MAGICAL/FANTASY SETTINGS– INSIDE A PAINTING

In a recent production we had characters jump "into" a painting as the scene changed from a park to an animated country setting. As they jumped, the lights went out. When the scene came back up the actors had changed into their country setting costumes and started the scene in the exact place and pose to simulate that the jump had just been completed (diagram 7.6).

Diagram 7.6

Note: Because this scene change required quick costume changes, we incorporated ensemble actors into the scene change and had them bring out the tea table and chairs, and then a tablecloth. They did some wonderful improvisation to stretch the scene change out to allow the actors the extra time they needed.

MAGICAL/FANTASY SETTINGS– UNDER THE SEA

Underwater scenes can be fun to create; use a plain blue backdrop, or patterned paper with bubbles on it, then add coral, seaweed, fish, treasure chests, and any number of other items with either cardboard pieces leaning against it or paper images fastened to it. Another option I used at a summer camp was a plastic tablecloth with all the underwater fish on it. In addition to being a great backdrop for skits, the campers loved having their photos taken in front of it! One other "special effect" that can be used is a bubble machine (or even someone behind a set piece with a bubble gun) to create real bubbles for some scenes.

MAGICAL/FANTASY SETTINGS –NORTH POLE / SANTA'S WORKSHOP

Many Christmas productions with children involve the North Pole or Santa's workshop in some scenes. You don't have to have an "outdoor" look, although a plain blue backdrop can be used to make a lovely outdoor winter scene with white paper "hills" and some snow covered mountains or trees added. To create the inside of Santa's workshop, a few simple flats with various toys and workshop "supplies" painted on them can be used, with an outdoor scene with trees and snow painted on the reverse side for later scenes. It's just as convincing to have a big Christmas tree upstage center that can be used for both indoor and outdoor scenes and utilize props and rolling carts to create the rest of your scene.

MAGICAL/FANTASY SETTINGS– ENCHANTED OR ANIMATED PLACES WITH ANIMALS

In most children's theatre productions, magical places will not be scary, but "enchanted". Costuming can help to create the scene more than the set pieces, but for a simple "animated" look for your set, you can find various free images and clip art cartoon pieces online to print out and attach to your cardboard flats. If you have a little bit of money some of these can be made into poster sized images at local print shops (look for when they have 20% off sales on poster/banner art and it becomes much more affordable!).

Another option is to use a document camera or overhead projector to make the image bigger on your backdrop flat or free standing cardboard. It takes some time to draw and paint the image, but it can result in a great animated look (diagrams 7.7 and 7.8). (This method works for other set pieces as well)

Diagram 7.7

Diagram 7.8

Chapter Eight

HOMEMADE INDOOR PROPS

Over the years it was necessary to create some props from nothing – usually items that were either hard to find or expensive to buy. While thrift stores and garage sales are wonderful resources to find items (along with various online sites like Ebay and Amazon), they are still a "hit or miss" adventure. There are times when a certain prop is needed, and it can be created using a strange combination of household items and some creativity.

INDOOR PROPS –

- old fashioned radios (big and small)
- old fashioned radio station microphone
- laundry cart from wagon
- snow globe
- cardboard toy blocks
- covered books and magazines
- clothesline with assorted items
- barrels of ale and gin
- assorted documents

INDOOR PROPS – OLD FASHIONED RADIOS

To make an old fashioned table top radio from the 40s era, all you need is cardboard, black duct tape, and a thick black marker. Start by cutting out two pieces of cardboard in the shape of a half oval – they should be about a foot tall and 10-12 inches wide (see diagram 8.1) Then cut a strip of cardboard that will reach from point A on the diagram up and around the top of the oval and down to point B – this strip should be 3-4 inches wide (diagram 8.2).

Diagram 8.2

Diagram 8.1

Line up the two half curved pieces and fasten one end of the long strip to each edge (this strip will be the "wall" of your radio). Slowly work your way around the top, using black or brown duct tape to attach the strip (see diagram 8.3). Be sure to keep the edges of your duct tape even so that it looks more like the radio's wood as opposed to pieces of tape thrown on it. Run one more thin piece of duct tape along the bottom of the flat bottom edge. When taped together, you can then draw a big circle for the speaker (I traced a cool whip cover for a perfect circle). Using a ruler or piece of cardboard, draw tiny lines in perpendicular fashion across the circle for a speaker "look" and then two circles in each corner for your knobs (diagram 8.4). You can also glue real wooden knobs on if you'd prefer.

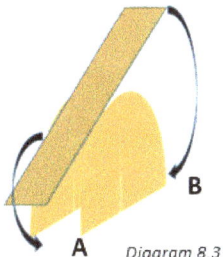 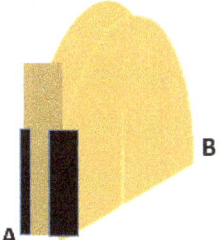 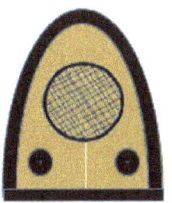

Diagram 8.3 *Diagram 8.4*

If you prefer a large sized radio that sits on the floor, you'll need either bigger pieces of cardboard (with curved pieces about three feet high), or a small table or shelving unit that curves at the top. Cut cardboard pieces that fit over the curved end pieces and cover them with paper or contact paper that looks like wood grain. Cut square pieces that cover the sides and attach all pieces to the edge of the table. Add speakers and knobs using the directions in prior section. (diagram 8.5).

 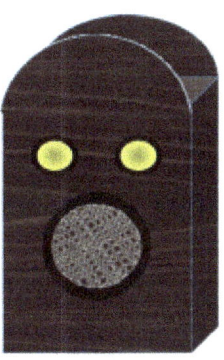

Diagram 8.5

Diagram 8.6

INDOOR PROPS – RADIO STATION MICROPHONE

Some shows require an old fashioned radio station microphone – ones that were big in the 1930s and 1940s. If you have access to a mic stand, you can draw out just the top piece shown in diagram 8.6 on poster or foam board and attach it to the mic stand with black duct or electrical tape. If you don't have a mic stand, you can create your own with a Styrofoam base (painted black). Take a wooden dowel—also painted black—and stick into the base until steady. You might need some tape or a glue gun to secure. Then proceed to make the top and attach to the dowel in the same manner (diagram 8.6). Here's one I had created for an old version of *Annie* – WSEG was an actual NYC station back in the 30s.

. . .

INDOOR PROPS – LAUNDRY CART

In *Annie* there is a scene where Annie escapes the orphanage in a big rolling laundry cart. Having no access to one, I used a child's red wagon and transformed it into something big enough for her to kneel in. Be sure the wheels are well inflated and that it pulls easily.

If the wagon is older (like the one I used), I started by taping down a piece of cardboard into the wagon to cover the bottom to keep any rust stains away from actor clothing. I then proceeded to cover the outside and the handle with white duct tape. I used white foam board for the sides and the sign. When attaching the sign, be sure to allow for the wagon wheels. If the sign is taped too tightly and totally flush with the edge of the wagon, it will be hard to pull and turn the wheels without damaging the sign (diagram 8.7). Pulling the wagon in a somewhat straight line across the stage will also help to keep the wheels from ruining the sign.

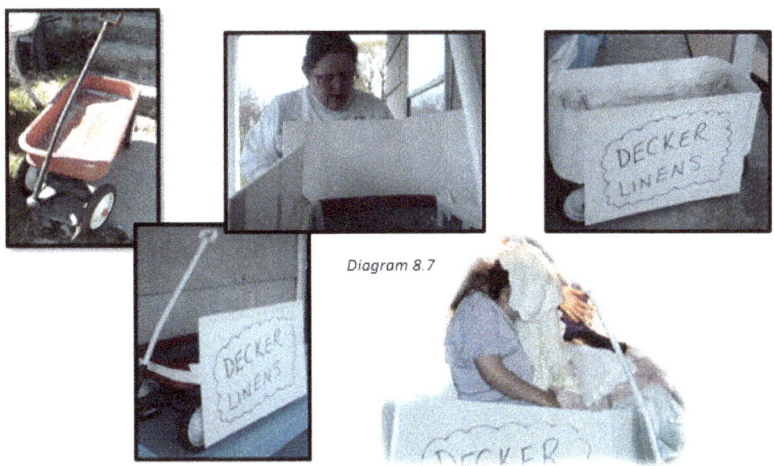

Diagram 8.7

INDOOR PROPS – SNOW GLOBE

For one show we used a snow globe as a prop. Since I didn't have access to the expensive ones with water and glitter, I purchased a plain plastic ball (sphere) at a local craft store for $4.00. Online I found a found a copyright free photo to use inside the globe.

After I saved the image, I copied the same image and formatted it with the "rotate horizontally" button on the computer; this gave me a mirror image, so that when I put them side by side I could print out a photo that was a mirror image when folded down the middle. I was able to also find some copyright free birds online and erased the background on them. (It would be just as easy to do the birds with a black Sharpie marker right over the photo). I folded the picture in half (diagram 8.8), then taped the four corners to the inside of one half of the plastic empty clear ball before snapping the other half on.

I then glued a roll of black duct tape (just as easy to use a big piece of styrofoam), and fastened the plastic sphere with the glue. When dry, it looked just like a cathedral from far away (diagram 8.9).

(fold mirror image in half)

Diagram 8.8

View of snowglobe front and back

Diagram 8.9

INDOOR PROPS – CARDBOARD TOY BLOCKS

Years back I did a children's theatre production where the setting took place in a school room for toys. Along with the help of the cast, who colored the pictures, we used cardboard, colored pictures and letters, duct tape, and milk crates to create big toy "blocks" that cast members could sit on and stand on when needed. When put together the four blocks spelled out "TOYS," and while separated across the stage they offered some color and flexibility in the simple set.

For each block, you need five squares of cardboard that cover the top and sides of a milk crate; remember to leave a little extra room so that they can taped together at all the seams (don't worry about the bottom). For each block I used three colored pictures and two letters. Pictures were used on the top, and then pictures and letters were used on opposite sides of the block. For example, block one might have a picture of a clown on the top of the block (audience will not see this picture, so I used any that might not have been colored in as carefully), and the four sides in order had the letter "T," a picture of a doll, the letter "A," and a picture of a flower. All pictures and letters were glued on before assembling.

To assemble, start with two squares that will make your top and first side. Tape seams lightly at first (I used scotch tape to hold it together while I was sure it was going to fit), and then duct tape all seams (diagram 8.10). I used WHITE cardboard so that the pictures showed up well with red or black letters and red duct tape. When finished, they could be lifted off of the milk crate for storage or given to various cast members as a memento when the show was over.

Here is what one block looks like, along with them all together:

Diagram 8.10

INDOOR PROPS – COVERED BOOKS AND MAGAZINES

One item that should be in your general prop inventory is a stack of plain brown covered books and a couple of magazines to fit a time period. Most of the books can be thin hardcovers – the subject matter makes NO difference as they will just be plain brown books that can used in ANY production. Lay each book opened and flat on the table on top of a plain brown grocery bag. Cut the bag out, allowing an extra couple of inches along the sides and top and bottom. At the top and bottom of the book cut a "U" section down closer to the spine of the book (diagram 8.11). Start by folding over the top and bottom folds to the inside and tape down. Fold the outside flaps in as well and tape. BE SURE TO ALLOW A LITTLE EXTRA MARGIN SO THAT YOU CAN CLOSE THE BOOK. If you tape it too tightly when the book is open, it will possibly rip or not close all the way. Start with ONE side of the book, and then CLOSE the book and fold paper on other side (diagram 8.12). Open it again and then tape second side.

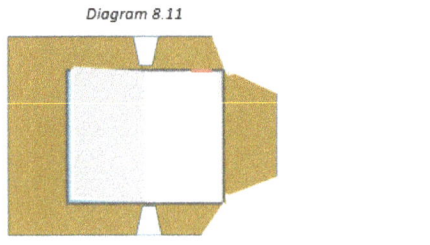
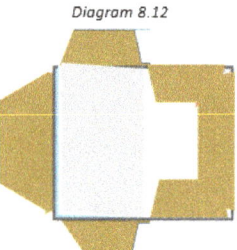

For magazines, it's really only the covers you need to worry about. If you search online, you can find copyright free images of old magazine covers and ads from almost any era. Just print one out and attach it to the front of your magazine. I tape the seam and edges to make sure it's secure.

INDOOR PROPS – INDOOR CLOTHESLINE

All that is needed are various pieces of fabric in different colors and textures attached to a piece of rope or clothesline with clothespins (use the old fashioned kind – not the ones with metal). Use bright colors to help them "pop" and add some contrast to the flats or backdrops (diagram 8.13).

If the clothesline needs to be set up and taken down several times, fasten it on one end just off stage to the top of a flat, and then put a clip on the other end; this is easy to pull out and attach to a wooden slat on a bench onstage (or it could be clipped to the top of another flat on stage). Being able to have it assembled and hidden just off stage makes for an easy scene change (diagram 8.13).

Diagram 8.13

For the same prop in a studio location, it was easy to just tie the clothesline to the tops of the black curtain being used as the backdrop (diagram 8.14).

Diagram 8.14

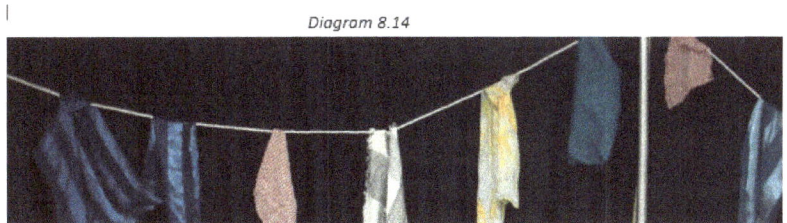

INDOOR PROPS – BARRELS OF ALE FOR A PUB

In one production we had an old English tavern, so we wanted to show barrels of gin, rum, and ale without having the big barrels on stage. Two options are to make them two dimensional as part of the front of the bar (diagram 8.15), or find smaller cardboard cylinders at a local craft store and cover them with wood patterned paper. Letters can either be put on with marker or cut out and glued on the end of each "mini barrel." I mounted them in and taped them together so they could sit on top of the bar (diagram 8.16).

Diagram 8.15

Diagram 8.16

INDOOR PROPS – OLD DOCUMENTS

For some shows you may need to have a prop such as an old newspaper, a birth certificate, or a contract. It's easy to find various images that are copyright free online and create your own documents that look more authentic. To create an older looking piece of paper, use either a parchment or tan colored paper to print on, or do a page design with the parchment texture and color to print out. You can also stain regular paper by dipping a paper towel in coffee or tea and smudging it on the white paper. Leave it in the sun to dry (diagram 8.17).

Diagram 8.17

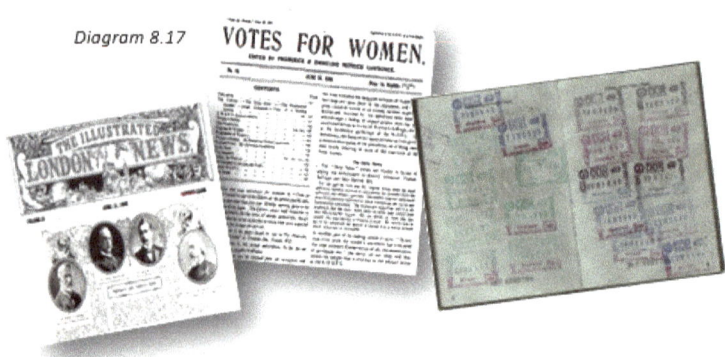

Chapter Nine
HOMEMADE FOOD PROPS

FOOD

- store bought fake food
- cheese
- steak
- Cakes (2)
- box of fudge
- fancy tarts
- french fries

FOOD - STORE BOUGHT FAKE FOOD
Note: Over the years I purchased a few key pieces of "fake food" to use repeatedly. I added a piece or two at a time to keep costs down. Fake fruit can be found at most dollar stores; fake bread and cheese cost a bit more, but are usually easy to find at local craft stores. I also found some fake hamburgers, hot dogs, and chicken legs at a local pet supply store – from far away, dog "chew toys" look quite realistic! Keep

your food items stored in a bin together for repeated use over time. To make some of your own, try these suggestions:

FOOD – CHEESE

To create realistic looking wheels of cheese, all you need are pieces of styrofoam from a local craft store. Paint them either yellow, orange, or red, and you have some easy and convincing cheese (diagram 9.1). Be sure NOT to use spray paint as it will damage the styrofoam.

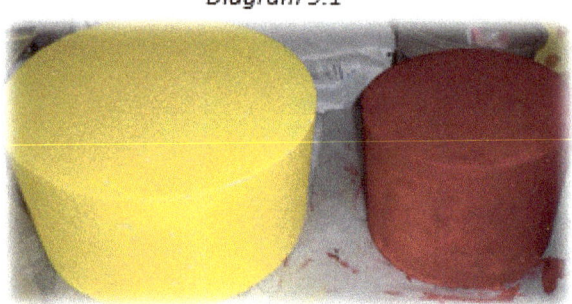

Diagram 9.1

FOOD – STEAK

Start with two pieces of Styrofoam (approximately 5x7 or 8x10) that are an inch or less in thickness. Use a boxcutter to trim the edges to create a "steak" shape. Paint both pieces red and use white paint for marbling.

Diagram 9.2

FOOD – CAKES

One cake is made by stacking two white round styrofoam pieces together; use a glue gun or a strong craft glue to ensure a firm adhesive bond. In addition, glue the bottom tier right onto the platter so that it won't move at all. Using various silk flowers, remove the flower petals from the stems (they just pull off if you are gentle). Arrange them around the cake and use a straight sewing pin to stick through the flower and into the Styrofoam (diagram 9.3). We used this as a food item in *Cinderella* for the royal cooks to present to the king and queen, and then it was held during the dance and held up wonderfully.

Diagram 9.3

For another cake for the same occasion, I used a plastic margarine container and painted it white. I then used a glue gun to attach it to a silver tray from the dollar store, and completed the look with black paint used for the frosting (diagram 9.4).

Diagram 9.4

FOOD – BOX OF FUDGE

Take either a block of wood or tape together a couple of empty pudding boxes and cover them with silver paper. Create a fancy "label" on the computer and glue it to the side (diagram 9.5).

Diagram 9.5

FOOD – FANCY TARTS

SETS ON A SHOESTRING

I created two types of "tarts" or fancy pastries using empty applesauce containers and cardboard egg cartons (the bottom half turned upside down). Paint the egg cartons pink and let them dry. Then apply some white paint to the top of the egg carton pastries to serve as whipped cream, and glue a small black pom pom to the top to resemble a raisin or piece of chocolate (or use a red pom pom for a cherry).

For the other "tarts", paint the applesauce containers pink (strawberry) and yellow (lemon). Let dry. Use black paint around the bottom rims, on the top, and down the side creases to reflect chocolate icing. While the paint is still wet, sprinkle a little glitter on the top. Put both these and the egg carton pastries on silver trays from the dollar store and use a glue gun to fasten (diagram 9.6).

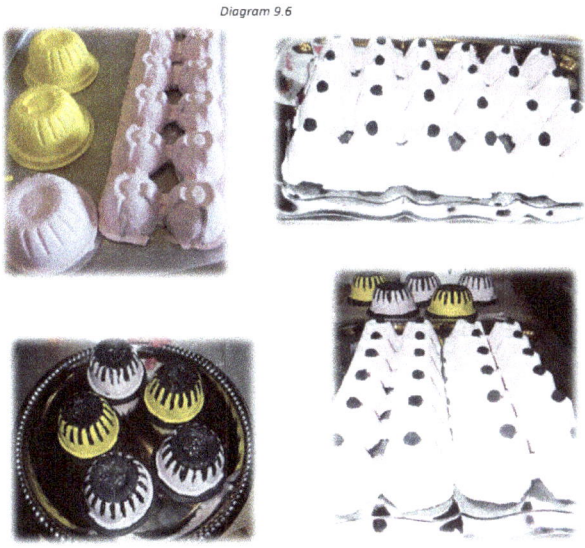

Diagram 9.6

FOOD – FRENCH FRIES

Use some cheap yellow sponges from the dollar store and a pair of pinking shears or scrapbook scissors. Cut the sponges into French fry strips and the scissors will make them appear to be crinkle cut fries (diagram 9.7). Use a glue gun to attach to a silver tray (or plate, depending on your use). If you want a few loose ones to have for the actor to use during a scene to simulate eating, leave a little "pocket" in your glued heap where they won't fall off as the tray is carried. From far away these look like the real thing!

Diagram 9.7

Chapter Ten
HOMEMADE OUTDOOR PROPS

OUTDOOR PROPS –

- pail of water
- lamp post
- kites on dowels
- rooftop chimneys with pipes

OUTDOOR PROPS – PAIL OF WATER

Several productions called for a pail of water to be spilled or dumped out. Since glitter is extremely hard to clean up and gets everywhere, use pieces of fabric attached to the bottom of the pail. I chose blue fabric with texture and glitter on the fabric and proceeded to cut it into lots of thin strips three to four feet in length. Attach each one with gray duct tape to the bottom of a gray pail (diagram 10.1). When "dumped", the fabric gave the impression of water that was moving – much more effective than glitter, and easily replaced into the pail for the next performance! Another option is to use blue crepe streamers instead of fabric strips.

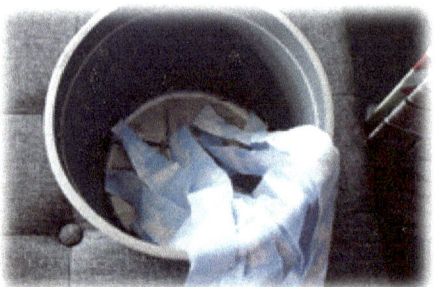
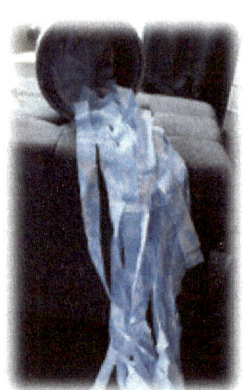

Diagram 10.1

OUTDOOR PROPS – LAMP POST

For two different productions I needed old fashioned lamp posts. After pricing them at about $80 each, knew that I had to come up with an alternative homemade version.

In making props, I learned over the years that one helpful tip is to look at the SHAPES involved and brainstorm on items that might work as that shape. In looking at a lamp post, I saw the top section, the long middle section, and the base at the bottom. The middle was easy – I knew I need a cylinder shape. I priced PVC piping, but even that was a little out of my price range. And then a good friend mentioned that she had cardboard tubes at work that I could have for nothing. She runs an awning company, and the fabrics come into the shop on cardboard tubes that can be anywhere from four to twelve feet long. I felt like I had hit the mother lode! I stopped by and picked up several six foot tubes and had my "middle" section for no cost. After a coat of black paint, it was set to go!

Diagram 10.2

The base section I knew had to be stable enough to hold up the prop, but also light enough to move easily. I finally found the perfect solution at Walmart with a heavy duty plastic wastebasket. It was light enough that I could still cut a hole with a boxcutter for the cardboard tube to slide into, but heavy and tall enough to provide a strong base and LOOK like a lamp post base you'd find outside (diagram 10.2).

The top proved to be a bit of a challenge for a couple of days, and then I realized that the perfect SHAPED item was a large take out container for Chinese food. I stopped by a local store and they gave me a few free ones, and I traced the bottom and sides onto a piece of cardboard. Cutting out four sides and the bottom, I gently taped them together to see if the size would work. Discovering that it would, I then placed the the four taped side pieces on a piece of cardboard to then trace the top piece. For the sides, I then cut out the middle of each piece, leaving only about a half inch along the edges remaining. I used black electrical tape to cover all the individual pieces – four sides, and the top and bottom pieces.

I then found that plastic transparency sheets worked PERFECTLY as "fake" glass, and cut three pieces to fit three sides – I taped them onto the back of three of the sides, and then proceeded to put the whole thing together with black electrical tape (diagram 10.3).

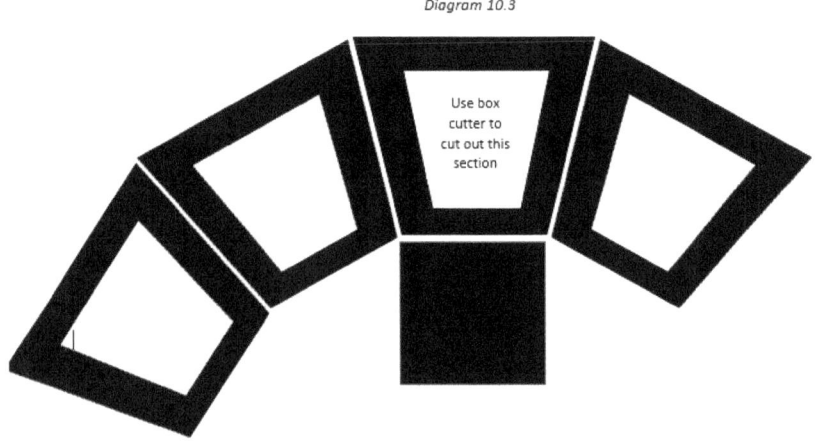

Diagram 10.3

I left the fourth side "window" open to allow the placement of a battery operated tea light to be placed inside. To top it off, I had found a couple of wooden ornaments at a thrift store for fifty cents each, and proceeded to tape those to the top (diagram 10.4).

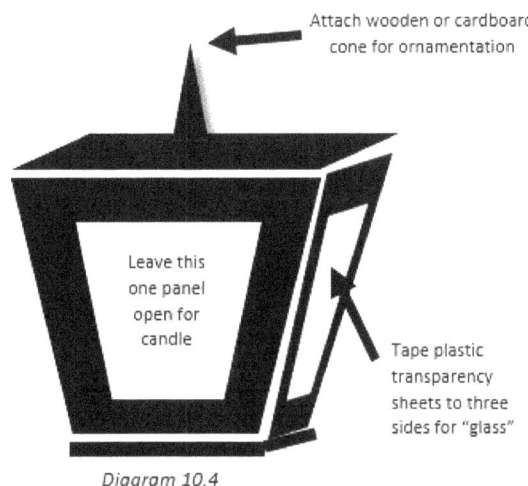

Diagram 10.4

In the end, I had two beautiful lamp posts that ended up costing me under $5.00 each to make (diagram 10.5).

Diagram 10.5

OUTDOOR PROPS – KITES ON DOWELS

In one production we needed kites that appeared to be flying. In a party supply catalog I was able to find a dozen paper kites at a reasonable price, and then had the cast proceed to decorate them with markers.

Once kites were decorated, a thin piece of wooden dowel was taped across the back from point to point (you can see the dowel through the kite in diagram 10.6). A longer thin dowel was then attached to the smaller one right in the center and secured with white duct tape. The dowel was strong enough to support the weight of the kite but still curved down as it was held. Cast members were able to wave the dowel back and forth to give the illusion that the kites were flying in the breeze.

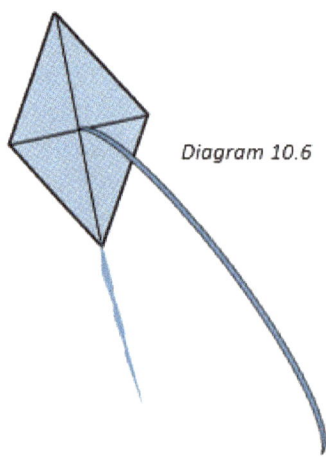

Diagram 10.6

OUTDOOR PROPS – ROOFTOP CHIMNEYS WITH FURNACE PIPES

To create a "rooftop" scene complete with chimneys and furnace pipes, refer back to the section on making toy blocks on page 63. The procedure is the same for assembly in terms of cutting and taping the cardboard to fit over milk crates. For this production we used one milk crate by itself and then two others taped together to create a longer chimney that people could walk over. Once covered with cardboard, we found brick patterned paper to cover them with. I then went to Home Depot and found thin metal duct pieces for about a dollar each and taped them to the piece for the "smoke" stacks (diagram 10.7)

To create just a tall chimney that someone could "hide" inside, use either one of the cheap trifold display boards that you can find at the dollar store or a large cardboard box with one side removed. Cover the whole thing with patterned brick paper and have someone crouched down behind it. They can then stand up and appear to be coming OUT of the chimney.

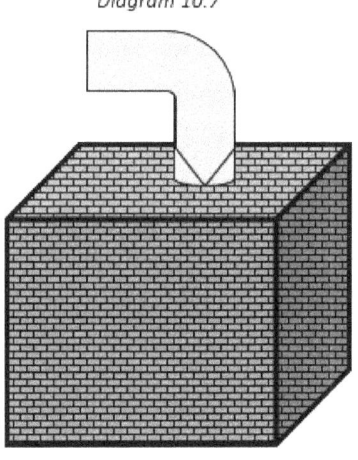

Diagram 10.7

Chapter Eleven
HOMEMADE FANTASY / MAGICAL PROPS

FANTASY / MAGICAL PROPS --

- carousel
- Cinderella's coach
- Oz door
- crystal ball
- fire ball
- cauldron
- magic Fireplace
- nursery toy box
- chimney sweep brushes
- chocolate waterfall
- small Machine

FANTASY / MAGICAL PROPS – CAROUSEL

I knew that I wanted a merry go round that my actors could both ride on and then leave; I also knew that I needed it to be small and easy to move on and off the stage. Several students with art backgrounds drew the horses onto cardboard and painted them to look like carousel horses at a carnival (diagram 11.1). We then glued thin ribbon around the dowel in a diagonal fashion to make the "pole" look striped. The pole was then taped to the back of the horse (both sides were painted, but the tape covered up a bit of the design on the back side).

For the "base" of the carousel, several pieces of cardboard were attached to form a "V" shape from the front of the carousel back to the two sides, along with a base piece along the floor to hold it up. It was then painted white and decorated (diagram 11.2).

Diagram 11.1

Diagram 11.2

The top of the carousel was a huge golf umbrella which a crew member held while facing backwards to obscure his face. We bought battery operated lights and attached them to the umbrella top.

When it was time for the scene, the base was placed on the designated spot and the tech person stood in the middle holding the umbrella high over his head, turning it slowly with the lights blinking. The four actors held their horses and rode around the inside edges moving their horses up and down slightly as you see on a carousel ride. They then stepped off and continued to "ride" their horses across the countryside. To finish the effect, we played a carousel ride sound effect in the background (diagram 11.3).

Diagram 11.3

FANTASY PROPS – CINDERELLA'S COACH

We used an actual sulky (a two wheeled buggy used in harness racing) with lots of tulle and orange Christmas lights to make it shine. Wheel decorations were made from cardboard circles. After glueing fancy ribbon on them we taped them to the spokes of the actual wheels. We dressed four cast members as white horses and they pulled the carriage (diagram 11.4).

Diagram 11.4

If you have no access to a vehicle Cinderella can SIT in, then use cardboard and cut out a big pumpkin shape with a "window" for her to look out. It could be mounted on one of the costume racks (using just the bottom half) and then pulled by Cinderella as she walked behind it. It could also be left as a flat piece of cardboard with a couple of loops taped to the back that Cinderella could hold as she carried it across the stage. Decorate either option with pretty lights and orange paint and it will be convincing (diagram 11.5).

Diagram 11.5

FANTASY / MAGICAL PROPS – DOOR TO OZ

As was stated earlier, having a an actual door when doing smaller and simple sets is not always practical. However, there are still ways to create the illusion of a door ON stage when needed. In a recent production, the doorman stood behind a costume rack that had a half door made from cardboard taped on the bottom. To cover up the opening we used Kelly green silk table runners from the dollar store and hung them from the top of the rack. They reached all the way down to the bottom of the door and the doorman just stuck his head out (diagram 11.6).

To hang the sign that said "bell out of order – please knock," we used an binder clip at the top of the half door (about waist level for him). The sign was on a string that was already hanging on the rear side of the set piece, so all he had to do was swing it around to the front.

When Dorothy and her friends made it in to see Oz, we added a sign that said "OZ" by hanging it along the top of the costume rack. We also had green battery operated Christmas lights blinking as OZ spoke behind the curtain. It was a simple solution for not having a door (diagram 11.6).

Diagram 11.6

FANTASY / MAGICAL PROPS – CRYSTAL BALL

Using another round plastic ball from the local craft store, I took some shiny silver mylar paper and crinkled it up to fill the inside. I then painted a styrofoam ring black, and used a glue gun to attach the two.

Diagram 11.7

FANTASY / MAGICAL PROPS – BALL OF FIRE

In one scene of a recent production, a witch throws a "fire" ball in the air. If you can't find a fake fire ball online, buy an orange stress ball or dog toy at a local dollar store, and then some gold shiny wrapping bows. I cut the bows into strips and used craft glue dots to attach to the ball (diagram 11.8). The end result from the audience perspective was convincing enough while staying well within budget.

Diagram 11.8

FANTASY / MAGICAL PROPS – CAULDRON

There are several options for creating a cauldron. One is to buy one all done from a Halloween party story – if you are just looking for a table top size you can usually find one under ten dollars. A bigger one will cost more.

If you are looking for just a shape that you can lean against a backdrop flat, a cauldron is easy to draw and paint on cardboard. You can also add a tab at the bottom of the piece and create a second support tab if you want it to be free standing (diagram 11.9).

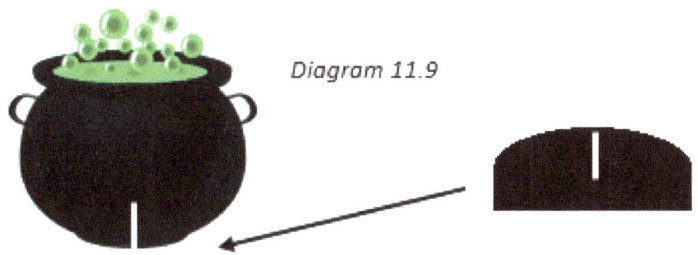

Diagram 11.9

If you'd like something a little bigger and more three dimensional, you can use a rolling costume rack and have the top bar at a lower height. Cut and paint your black cauldron out of cardboard and the buy a few feet of small chain link from a hardware store and duct tape one end of the chain to the back of the cauldron and the other to the top of the bar (diagram 11.10).

Diagram 11.10

FANTASY / MAGICAL PROPS – MAGIC FIREPLACE

In a recent production we wanted to show a letter being ripped up and thrown into a fireplace before magically floating up the flue. The first task was to use cardboard (either an old box or cut big pieces and tape together) to make the front part and the mantel of the fireplace. After that a second piece of cardboard is cut and placed behind the first to create the back of the fireplace (to give it a slightly three dimensional look). Fold the edges of the back pieces into two flaps that will attach to the front piece while leaving 4-6 inches of space between the front and back pieces. In our production the students covered the front of the fireplace with marble patterned paper, and then the back piece with brick paper. There should be a gap at the top of the back piece that is NOT taped to anything – this should be high enough behind the first piece so that it's not seen from the audience. This is the opening that the "letter" will magically disappear to (diagram 11.11).

You then need a narrow box (or you can make one from cardboard) with a cardboard fire log (again, you can either use wood patterned paper or draw/paint a wooden log) taped to the front. This piece is placed into the fireplace leaving a small gap between the back of the box and the back wall of the fireplace. When a letter is thrown into the fire, it should be placed into the little box behind the log.

In the meantime, you will need a duplicate letter taped together in pieces and attached to a piece of fishing line. The whole clump should then be placed in the fireplace BEHIND the log and little box for the ripped up version of the letter. The fishing line should feed up the fireplace flue and over the top of the open edge to the back (note: tape a piece of paper or a paper clip to the end behind the chimney so it's easy to find and pull!). When it's time to create the "magic" of the letter going up the chimney, a tech person sits behind the fireplace and slowly pulls the letter up and over the open edge (diagram 11.12). The effect looks amazing from the audience!

Diagram 11.11

Diagram 11.12

FANTASY / MAGICAL PROPS – NURSERY TOY BOX

In the same manner that the letter goes up the chimney with fishing line, the toys find their way back into the toy box also with the help of invisible fishing line. In our production we used an old trunk as the toy box, but you could use any little closet or shelving unit. It needs to be big enough for someone to hide behind it. For our production we tied fishing line to a rag doll, a teddy bear, and a wooden train. We attached clips to the end of each piece so that it was easy to locate. The teddy bear and the doll literally flew back into the toy box as the fishing line was fed through the space near the lid's hinges! The train rode off the stage on its own as the fishing line pulled it in behind the toy box.

Diagram 11.13

FANTASY / MAGICAL PROPS – CHIMNEY SWEEP BRUSHES

For this project you'll need cardboard, black paint, black plastic drinking straws (I got them on Amazon and paid about fifteen dollars for two huge packs – we had about fifty left over after making a dozen sweep brushes and used them for "repairs" during the production. You'll also need either wooden dowels or plastic dance canes. The dowels are a bit cheaper, but you'll have to paint them. The plastic dance canes ran about fifteen dollars for a dozen, and we just had to use black sharpie on the two ends which had white caps. You'll also need glue guns and lots of glue sticks for assembly!

For each brush, you'll need to cut out two round cardboard circles about six inches in diameter (I used margarine and cool whip container lids to trace). Use 25 straws for each cardboard round (50 for each brush). Using a glue gun, attach the straws around the edges as shown (diagram 11.14). Once dry, take two completed cardboard rounds and glue them together with all the straw ends on the inside. You can either paint the cardboard black after glueing or before. Only the outside needs to be painted.

You'll then take a piece of cardboard about three inches wide and wrap it around the end of the cane so that it overlaps a bit. Tape to hold the shape in place, and then remove the cane to paint black and secure with black duct tape or a glue gun (we used tape for this one). You'll then glue one end of this tube to the middle of the cardboard round of brushes as shown (diagram 11.15).

Diagram 11.14

Diagram 11.15

You now have a choice on assembly. You can attach the brush section to the cane by sliding the tube part snugly over one end and then use black duct tape or glue to permanently attach. Others keep the canes and brushes as separate pieces for storage, just taping them during production and then removing them after a show for storage again. I chose the first method described for a more secure fit as I didn't want the ends of the brush coming off while dancing. However, you'll need some extra room for storage as they do take up a fair amount of space if you have quite a few of them.

Diagram 11.16

Here's one photo that shows one of the chimney sweeps and a brush during production (diagram 11.16) The brushes held up incredibly well and were light enough to throw during choreography. Occasional straws fell out, but they were easy to repair or just leave out. The overall look was fabulous!

. . .

FANTASY / MAGICAL PROPS – CHOCOLATE RIVER

In a *Willy Wonka* production, there is nothing more "magical" than the chocolate river, but trying to create it can be challenging (*especially* on a tight budget). I used two cardboard flats with patterned paper depicting a big stone wall with ivy; for the river itself, I hung a brown vinyl tablecloth in between the flats with strips cut along the bottom so that Augustus could "fall" through to the back. To give a more three dimensional look, we had a fan backstage blowing on it so that it looked more like it was moving. As an added bonus, a talented student created a computer image of an animated chocolate river. He brought in a projector and the river actually appeared to be flowing down through the audience. It was a striking special effect (diagram 11.17).

Diagram 11.17
animated computer image
by Ben Blease

In a more recent production, we used two big pieces of chocolate brown fabric and had dancers carry each corner to create the river. As they danced the river literally came to life and swallowed up Augustus to carry him offstage.

FANTASY / MAGICAL PROPS – SMALL MACHINE

Starting with a cardboard box, I covered it with two silver gift bags from the dollar store (remove handles, cut down one seam, and either cut out bottom or undo the tape to open it up flat). I then used shiny silver duct tape to attach two silver balloon paperweights to the top.

To add a little "bling" I also taped a dollar store light stick that turned on and off with the press of a button (diagram 11.18).

Diagram 11.18

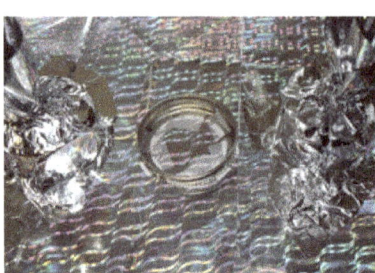

Chapter Twelve

HOW MUCH SHOULD THE CAST HELP?

This is a question that comes down to your philosophy as a director. There are pros and cons to having help in creating a set. On the one hand, it's a lot of work even doing SIMPLE sets and sharing the burden makes life a LOT easier for a director. However, in relinquishing that control you also have to accept that things might not have a "perfect" look—especially if working in children's theater when it's kids helping with the set.

    I have been a part of community theater productions where the cast would all work for hours to paint sets and props, only to find that the director had redone some of the work because it didn't look "good" enough. The result was a cast who felt that they had wasted their time or that they weren't valued at all. While the set looked great, the morale in the cast suffered. In some high schools I've seen students denied the opportunity to serve as student light or set designers because professionals were necessary to create the "perfect" look. In my early years of directing I'd go to see these shows and leave with the "set envy" I mentioned at the beginning of the book. I also felt sorry for those students who might have learned countless lessons in leadership and collaboration, but instead were limited to serving as only helpers.

While I have no moral judgements on these productions, I realized that I was not in a position to have "perfect" sets with my budget. In addition, if I was going to have cast members and family help, I needed to allow them the ownership of what they were doing and NOT touch things up after they had left for the day. In doing so I've watched cast camaraderie grow and I've learned that it's more about the process than the "image" at the end that was important to my own directing style.

That being said, I also learned that I didn't like huge "armies" coming to help, as it became very stressful for everyone asking for guidance and directions all at the same time. I would usually schedule designated "set" days when I would have lists of items that needed to be completed with general directions on how to proceed for each. I also tried to keep my "helpers" down to under a dozen on any given day so that it allowed all to be productive instead of waiting on my being able to get them started on a new project.

Diagram 12.1

In later years I actually had another cast mom assist a "technical" group of kids who didn't want to perform, but still wanted to be a part of the group. This group was a HUGE success and spent rehearsal hours working on various props and set pieces under the guidance of the cast mom and a student director.

One other job that is SO important to offer is that of student director. Over the years I have had several serve in this capacity, and while each one is different in the gifts they bring to the production, all of them were absolute blessings in the contributions they made. One year the student director might focus on keeping track of your endless lists and come to paint sets; another year they might block and direct a scene or two; still another year they might head up the "technical" group of kids or run the lighting for the show.....ALL of them sat in during auditions and helped with the casting—that alone allowed them to see the complex task of putting the pieces together in assembling a cast. In whatever capacity they end up serving, they will lighten your load and learn some important lessons in being a team leader. (There were a couple of years when no one expressed an interest, but I recommend that you offer the opportunity early on to an older and more experienced cast member who might want to try something different).

While I learned that smaller groups were more effective in putting the set *together*, I preferred the "army" at the other end when it was time to strike the set after the final performance. If you have a relatively large cast and a larger audience of family and friends, you'll find that most will stick around to help if you make the expectation known and stress the importance of the task being part of the overall theatre experience. No one likes the "diva" who takes off right after performing and leaves the clean up for everyone else! Many directors will remember these choices in future years when casting.

On set strike days, I come prepared with long lists of required tasks, from removing cardboard flats from frames and packing up props and costumes, to vacuuming the dressing room floor, and putting chairs away in the audience. I lay them out on the edge of the stage or ask a few trusted parents to supervise various sections. Most of my sets have been entirely taken down within an hour or two.

Whichever method you find works best for you – working alone or working with others, be sure to invite the cast members to share their gifts in various ways during production. While most love the acting more than anything, many of them have unique and individual talents that they are happy to share which add to the overall show. I had one student create a few beautiful costumes. Yet another took on doing the program and publicity posters. Another decided to take a break from acting one year and operated the lighting board for a show and helped with making props. In these examples, and many more, individuals took pride in sharing their talents and contributing as a valuable team member. These are lessons they will take with them into the future both on and off the stage!

Chapter Thirteen
THE USE OF LIGHTING AND SOUND

If you are reading this book, chances are you don't have a lot of resources available for fancy light or sound designs. I remember over the years being able to finally afford a spotlight, but before that the lighting was usually an "on" or "off" setting. If you are fortunate enough to have a spotlight with colored gels, you can help to create the setting with the touch of a button. Blue gels help to create night scenes, amber will add to morning, fire, or any "angry" scene, and green sets the mood for fantasy or alien creatures.

Sometimes you might perform in a location that allows a few spots on the stage to be better lit; for years I had four main "pockets" of light in addition to full lighting, so I was sure to do my blocking in those areas where the audience would be able to see the scene at its brightest. Other times you might block a performance one way, only to find when you arrive at the performance venue that the lighting will not accommodate your plan. Occasionally this resulted in changes to blocking just before a performance; whenever possible, visit the performance venue ahead of time so that last minute changes aren't needed.

Keeping a SIMPLE lighting design helps when you are trying to focus on teaching technique. If the only options for lighting are "on" and "off," then you need to find other ways to create the changes in time for any given setting. Sometimes it just relies on the actors on to convey what time of day or night it is, or to help convince the audience that the mood has just changed.

One resource that truly can help create the changes in mood and set the time frame is with the use of *music*. In some productions you might use a live pit, or all tracked music, or a combination of both. No matter what your source, music and sounds can help with your overall set design. For example, I recently did a simple production where the show began on a farm. I found royalty free sound effects of chickens and roosters on youtube and downloaded them as mp3 files, and then burned a CD with that and other royalty free sound effects.

Even with the lights on full, having the sound of crickets chirping and soft lullabies will help the audience believe it's evening. In Appendix B there are sites listed that will help you to find royalty free sounds and music, as well as a free music editing software program that allows you to learn how to shorten music clips and blend some together.

APPENDIX A – PHOTO CREDITS

All diagrams and most photos were created or taken by me.
Those photos taken by others are credited below:
Diagram 5.4 --Jackie Winters
Diagram 5.5 -- Ben Blease (window design)
Diagram 5.7 -- Jill Gupta
Diagram 6.3 --Alix French
Diagram 7.6 --Alix French (both images)
Diagram 8.7 --Rebecca Wenson
Diagram 11.3 --Alix French
Diagram 11.12 --Alix French
Diagram 11.13 --Alix French
Diagram 11.14 --Vicki Ferrari
Diagram 11.16 --Alix French
Diagram 11.17 --Jackie Winters (left image)
Ben Blease (right image)

APPENDIX B – USEFUL RESOURCES

Here are some of the resources I've used over the years:

- Uline – sheets of cardboard (I used the 40" x 60" size)
- Shindigz – patterned paper rolls
- Staples (copying / windows / banners)
- Awning stores – long tubes of ALL sizes (often at no cost)
- Pixabay - Online copyright free images/photos
- Wikimedia - Online copyright free images (some require attribution)
- Youtube - Royalty free sound effects. (be sure to look for royalty free!)
- Audacity - Free music editing software
- Amazon - various props listed throughout

ACKNOWLEDGMENTS

There are numerous people who helped to make this book a reality, and I am forever grateful to each of you:

To Rebecca Wenson for inviting me to Camp NaNoWriMo, and for your endless encouragement across the table as we wrote

To Christina Dunbar for your professional editing help and valued input

To beta readers Caitlin McEnroe and Beth Barshinger for your helpful suggestions and overall support

To Dr. Melissa Koberlein for your guidance and expertise along the pathway to indie publishing

To my Publishing for Writers classmates and GLVWG friends for your love and camaraderie as fellow authors

Finally, to my family — for being my source of love and inspiration every single day

ABOUT THE AUTHOR

Laurel Wenson's directing career spans fifteen years in children's theater productions. She has worked in homeschool co-ops, private studios, and school settings as both director and music director, and has designed and built simple cardboard sets for musicals, plays, skits, camps, and theater classes for children of all ages.

She recently took her final curtain call as a director, but continues to speak about children's theater in various settings. In addition to theater, Laurel has taught english classes to homeschoolers of all ages, and continues to do so through her online tutoring business *Lessons by Laurel*. She is currently working on her first contemporary young adult novel. Laurel lives in Pennsylvania with her husband, two daughters, and two cats.

You can learn more at laurelwenson.com

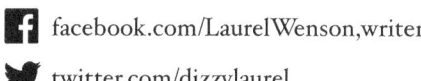

facebook.com/LaurelWenson,writer

twitter.com/dizzylaurel

www.ingramcontent.com/pod-product-compliance
Lightning Source LLC
Chambersburg PA
CBHW062023290426
44108CB00024B/2751